Making Your Mind Your Best Friend

A Handbook of Applied Spirituality

Baba Shuddhaanandaa Brahmachari

Sheema Publishing

Sheema Publishing, LLC
Portage, MI
Tel: 269-615-1648
Email: sheemapublishing@sbcglobal.net
Web site: www.naturalhealing.org

Previous 2003, 2006 editions titled:
Your Mind, Your Best Friend
Published by Stress Management Academy, Calcutta

ISBN-13 978-0-9790993-2-8
ISBN-10 0-9790993-2-3

An application to register this book for cataloging has been submitted to the Library of Congress.

1. Self-help. 2. Inspirational. 3. Spirituality. I. Title.
Printed in the United States of America
Cover design by: Sanjay Chakraborty

For the Seekers

In the Path of Light and Love

Baba Shuddhaanandaa Brahmachari

ACKNOWLEDGMENTS

I am indebted to the many devotees who shared their precious time and energy in making this book possible, particularly to Ann Shannon for transcribing the original tapes and editing each edition to make it a true companion for seekers of peace and love. My special thanks, too, to Haskell and Rae Fuller, Susan Berg, Connie Weaver, Marjorie Hilliard, and Ashis Khan for their dedication and feedback in the preparation of this edition.

Wayfarer, there is no way.
The way is made by walking.
There is no way to peace and happiness.
Peace and Happiness is the way.
– Buddha

CONTENTS

INTRODUCTION

What you hold in your hand is a spiritual gem, an unassuming, extraordinary medium of grace and healing, a cornerstone of spiritual practice for the sincere seeker. These materials were gathered and edited from the taped lectures of Baba Shuddhaanandaa Brahmachari, also simply called "Baba." They come straight from the purified heart of one of God's humblest servants. Do not take my word for it. Read the first reading, do the first exercises to discover the magnitude of what awaits you.

Here, Baba presents a new, core concept of the life of the spirit which brings an epiphany to many readers: making your mind your best friend. As Baba explains and as you begin to apply the principles, it becomes readily apparent that training your mind to become your best friend is more than wishful thinking. It involves much more than a simplistic loyalty to being positive for its own sake or for any utilitarian benefit. It does not repress any aspect, any experience of life. *Making Your Mind Your Best Friend* offers a universal, grounded, and compassionate response to the deepest human suffering. It traces the root cause of suffering to its source and provides the antidote: returning your mind to its ultimate reference point and resource, your enduring and sustaining context in a beneficent universe, in God. Taken to heart and applied, the practices contained here begin to calm the mind of its fears, its guilts and distortions.

I speak as a person with twenty years of meditative practice. My practice, as it was, simply was not enough. I had always had more than a minor visceral reaction to "positive thinking." As I understood and had seen it embodied, "positive thinking" was superficial and repressive. I felt compelled to be more honest, to penetrate the deeper and harsher complexities of being human. Over the decades, however, my own approach had reached its limit. My mind was collapsing in on itself. My ability to meditate, to practice at all, was withering. Rather than finding resolution and transformation, I was becoming less and less able to cope.

Mercifully, the mind responds to the concepts presented here. It responds naturally. The mind hungers for its true context. It surrenders. I cannot recommend *Making Your Mind Your Best Friend* enough to you. Working with these principles and practices can free you from the past. It can sustain you through any crisis of the moment. There is no need to be dominated by any mechanism of your mind, however entrenched. There is no need to feel oppressed by yourself, by life, or by circumstance. It is possible to let all of the joys and struggles of life come and go because you *know* that all is well. That possibility is not in the remote distance when you are working with these teachings.

Baba is a simple monk. He is a universal spiritual teacher. His only aspiration is to serve the living God in all who suffer, to faithfully serve his Divine Beloved. A master of himself and of devotional service to God, Baba is also a master of tender and tireless compassion. He is as committed to addressing the psychological and spiritual dilemmas of the West as to serving the poor in India, where he is a pioneer sustainable development leader in West Bengal. We, too, suffer, in the midst of abundance. Who does not suffer? What is impoverishment if not imprisonment in the illusion of our separation from God, from the absolute goodness and generosity of our own true being?

As Baba states, we have acquired our destructive habits of mind through many years of practice. Transforming them requires effort and persistence. I suggest that you cycle through the readings and practices many times over. Find a pace that is workable for you, which practices speak the most to your own nature. Be creative. I read it with a notebook, making lists of affirmations to use in my daily life. Before my husband died, he and I read the practices for each other, repeating certain phrases again and again as a part of our morning practice.

Sometimes, a practice may bring up what stands in the way of its realization. If that happens for you from time to time, I urge you to persist with the practice until you experience the deeper, truer reality.

Joy awaits you!
Ann Shannon
Editor

FROM THE AUTHOR

Radiant Spirits and Embodiments of Pure Joy,

I have been overwhelmed by the response from readers of the previous editions of *Making Your Mind Your Best Friend*, which was first published in India in 2003 with the title ***Your Mind Your Best Friend***. I have received letters from around the world about its power to inspire faith in one's own self and to open a practical understanding of the role of the mind in the path of the spirit. Many have written that they have found answers to their most unresolved questions about life and living. To me this indicates that the purpose *of Making Your Mind Your Best Friend* is being fulfilled through the grace of the Author of authors.

It has always been my most profound wish to have this book published in America and available to readers through major book stores. This hope has materialized with this new, expanded edition of *Making Your Mind Your Best Friend.* We have expanded the practices and added a new and timely chapter *Active Compassion and Global Transformation.* In this new chapter I invite the reader to contemplate how collective prayer and meditation offer immense potential for global transformation.

I pray that your hearts will be touched by these simple truths and that your ability to channel your energies toward a healthy body, mind, and the inner world of spiritual happiness will be nourished by these gentle reminders of the ultimate truth that you have always known in your spirit.

My love and prayers go out to all of you for a joyful journey home to your most beloved friend, the Blessed One who lives in the shrine of your own heart. May *Making Your Mind Your Best Friend* illumine your life and bring you peace and humility, love and gratitude for all the invaluable, infinite gifts of the Universe.

Baba Shuddhaanandaa
Kolkata
June 15, 2008

Reading, Day 1

YOUR ONE TRUE FRIEND

What God wants for you, first and foremost, is for you to find your one true friend in all the world. Your one true friend is your own mind which befriends you in all circumstances, a mind which always returns you to the ultimate truth and the infinite resources of your home in the Divine. Such a mind dispels the illusion of distance and separation from God. Such a mind returns, now and here, to the living presence of the Divine in all circumstances. Such a mind is anchored in the truth of its existence in God, in the instructions of the Holy Ones. Your one true friend is your mind that is ever rooted in the potentials and realities of your oneness with the Divine.

The more committed you are to making your mind your best friend, the more your mind becomes brilliant. It becomes lustrous. It opens to consciously receive the infinite blessings that are unfolding at every instant to direct you toward the home of your own spirit, which is one with God. It opens to give you greater blessings than you ever dreamed possible.

The enlightened masters of the world tell us that our best friend, first and foremost, must be searched for and found. So what do we do? We go about our daily lives searching, seeking a good friend for our protection, for our social living, for everything that helps us to subsist in the world. Finally, we realize it is very difficult to find a friend. After all, a friend is nothing but a mind . . . and a mind is the most unpredictable thing in this universe. You can never know at what moment even your best friend will suddenly turn into a hurtful stranger.

Who are we going to trust if we cannot trust our own mind? If we can't trust our own self, who are we going to trust? The spiritual journey, thus, is always centered around our own mind, our own self, our own being. We dig in our own field to discover reality and to test it.

If you are seeking and searching for a true friend who would be by your side when you are in danger, a friend who will understand your true need, then know your mind which listens to you. Know your mind which is disciplined through yoga, meditation, prayer, and spiritual practice. Know that which allows your mind to be in Divine contemplation, to be anchored in the Divine. That kind of mind is your true friend. That kind of mind sustains you through the turbulence and vagaries of life. It doesn't allow you to droop downward because you are suddenly faced with a dire situation.

Anything can happen to you externally. External circumstances are most unpredictable. We cannot predict what is going to happen, even in the next moment. Things outside of us, people outside of us, everything that is around us is changeable, inalterably unpredictable in its nature. That is nature.

We need to seek and find a true friend in this difficult, human state.

The only real solution is to befriend yourself. Make friends with your own mind first. Then seek friends outside. When you find your mind has become your true friend, you will be surrounded with friends. You won't have enough time to see all of your friends.

When we dwell in willingness, in appreciation, in thankfulness, in trust, in true friendship with ourselves, gradually we come to realize that if what we are working toward, if what we are hoping for, doesn't happen, then God is working toward some greater beneficence through whatever does happen. There is nothing to fear. There is nothing to be upset about. There is no reason to hold back from life. We move ahead freely, confidently, lovingly, befriending everybody around us, because we are always befriending our own self. We never create an enemy outside, because we never live with the enemy inside.

In that state of friendliness within, you are never a victim. There is no self-condemnation, there is no guilt, there is no question of blame, there is no depression. Your mind is more and more vibrant. It is buoyant. It moves naturally upward because it is light. It vibrates at a very high level. It attracts the ethereal vibrations of the holy saints and sages that are eternally available to all human beings. The words of the saints and sages, their inspiration, their grace are flowing out to you. Everything is available to you the moment you raise your mind and heart to that positive field. Ever so gradually, you absorb the graceful, eternal teachings. You grasp new, deeper meanings. You grow in awareness and consciousness. You come to understand the essence, you become the essence, of the eternal teachings.

Practice

1. Spend some time before the mirror, looking into your own eyes. Affirm that you are a radiant child of infinite light. See the beauty, the goodness, the love and light shining in your own eyes. Remind yourself: I am a child of the Infinite. I am creative and deeply good. I am an embodiment of love. I give love to everyone I meet. Tell yourself, "I love you and others love you," until you know it is true.

If it feels awkward and uncomfortable at first, and it probably will, persist until you authentically experience your own beauty and value shining back at you, until you feel what it means to love yourself. Make it real.

2. Standing at the mirror and looking into your own eyes, affirm that you are a blessing to your family and to society, that you are born to be successful and happy. Feel the glow of love in your own heart. Work on the plane of spiritual consciousness as well as on the physical plane. Look into your eyes without blinking and feel the calmness there. Remind yourself of your own inner and outer gifts until you feel inspired by them.

Reading, Day 2

THE UNIVERSAL JOURNEY

Our human journey is from lower truth to higher truth, from darkness and ignorance to light and wisdom, from fear of death to deathlessness. It is a journey through the mind, a journey which trains the mind, a journey which always returns the mind to its true, encompassing home in the unifying spirit. We do the basic work of that journey by making our mind our best friend, by continuously anchoring and re-anchoring ourselves in the ultimate truths of spirit.

We all carry the Divine seed in our hearts. In one who is awakened, however, that Divine essence is fully conscious, fully available. It is the extent to which we feel the presence of the Divine, the extent to which we see the world through the eyes of our innate

Divinity, that makes all the difference. The one who is awakened, the Buddha, is ever conscious of the pristine state within. He or she sees and relates to the world through the light of inner illumination.

That is why so many of us worship enlightened masters. We honor the Divine they have mastered and which they embody, because we ourselves are sparks of the Divine. In our own hearts, in the very core of our being, we recognize and long for a life of conscious union with our Divine source. We long for that life to be fully realized in ourselves.

It is nothing but a notion of our minds that God is somewhere else — in the heavens, deep in the clouds, far, far away from us — and that we need to call God to come to us, to bless us and rid us of our troubles. God is nowhere else. God is now and here. If you could squeeze all the religions of the world into one drop of wisdom, it would be: God is now and here . . . nowhere else.

The function of all religion and all spirituality is to bridge the illusory gap between the seeker and the Divine within, between the individual and the whole from which we are all inseparable.

No one creates this distance but us. The distance, the separation between us and God, the separation between us and all of Creation, is an illusion of the mind. That illusion may be stubborn. That illusion may be convincing. But it is also the source of all human misery, so penetrating the illusion each and every time it arises is a central, critically important practice of the sincere seeker.

We ourselves create the distance of our separation. That core illusion veils our consciousness like a darkened shroud. We are also the only ones who can begin to dispel its shadow.

The human mind is conditioned by eons of inherited patterns of perception and response, by our personal, existential ethos — those sets of attitudes and beliefs, or *samskaras*, that support survival in a given environment. All of these impressions are buried deep in the multiple layers of our subconscious mind. It takes time, perseverance, faith, inordinate compassion and commitment, to uproot and weed them all out.

Self awareness is the ancient, yogic path to liberation. Our minds are only marginally aware of ourselves. Through yoga, we collect ourselves, we return to now and here. Yoga brings us here, right now, to our experience at this instant, so that we are nowhere else. We cannot climb a mountain to reach God. We cannot walk a hundred or even a thousand miles to reach God. We cannot go to a church, mosque, or temple to reach God. We cannot go to the forest to find God. God can only be found in the truth of nearness. God is within us all.

That is the message of the wisdom of the *Vedas*, the most ancient of the world's spiritual literature. You are the children of immortality. You are inseparable from Ultimate Reality. You and Reality are One. You are indivisible from all that is. It is the *Dharma,* the duty and destiny of humankind, of every human soul, to realize that deeper, ultimate life.

Thus, we are blessed. We are blessed by all of the Great Ones who have gone before us. We are blessed by each instant, by each experience of our lives, leading us certainly and ultimately home. We know that. We always knew.

The teachers and guides of the soul come only to confirm it, to reaffirm it, to hammer the nail again so that it goes a little deeper, so that faith deepens, so that trust happens. We learn to move with trust, with faith, from head to heart, and to open our heart with single-pointed devotion. With love, befriending ourselves and all whom we meet, we move toward that one, encompassing reality, toward that One Truth, toward "The One without the second" spoken of in Vedic tradition.

Practice

1. Spend some time reflecting and writing on the process of your own unfolding life journey. Trace the major threads and themes of the evolution of your spirit from childhood until today. What have the driving forces been in your personal evolution of consciousness? How has your life been a movement from the lower to the higher, from fear to faith?

2. How have any experiences of your own lower nature, of darkness, of fear and pain, ultimately contributed to your turning more to the life of your spirit?

3. What still burdens you today? If those burdens were lifted, what would you have gained from having had them?

4. Reflect on the larger journey of human evolution in the same way you have examined your own life. How are we all on a collective journey?

5. Trace the thread of unfolding understanding and light in your life journey. What have been some of the major, determinant landmarks, the points of illumination and inspiration? Step back and see the delicate thread of light that has been emerging through your life experience.

Reading, Day 3

LIFT YOUR MIND WITH YOUR OWN MIND

Your mind is the instrument with which you are working, either to lower yourself or to uplift yourself, whether to bind yourself or to free yourself. All miseries come from the bondage of the untrained mind.

We are all entrapped by the creations of our own mind. We are all entangled in our own illusions. We are trapped in our projected thoughts, ideas, and concepts. It is only human to fall prey to the games of mind, to fall into self-deception.

A truly spiritual mind is always positive, always rooted in the expansive nature and capacities of the spirit. A truly spiritual mind is a trained mind. One of the ways by which you train your mind is to lift your mind with your own mind. Uplift yourself by yourself. Free yourself. Unfetter and unchain yourself. It is the mind which is in bondage. It is the mind which can unfetter and free itself. Lift yourself up. Lift to the higher realms of the spirit within you. That is the gateway to peace and happiness.

The ultimate state of human mind occurs when the mind becomes single-pointed and flows uninterruptedly toward its own origin in spirit, toward its intrinsic Divine potential.

That mind is your best friend; it is your greatest blessing. The blessing is not only to you individually, though. It is a blessing for all humanity, for the whole universe.

The mind that is your best friend is in a state of continuous, authentic celebration. It is ever in the present, ever celebrating the presence of the Divine.

The mind that is your best friend is a mind that looks for the deeper blessings behind all that is transient in nature. It sees the sun beyond the clouds of circumstance.

The mind that is your best friend is a positive, befriending mind that establishes itself in a state of yoga in the truest sense. This state of yoga yokes you. It unites you in communion with your indestructible Beloved; with that which is beyond fear, beyond anxieties, beyond all troubles and tribulations, beyond all negativity.

The mind that is your best friend is your positive, befriending mind that is at peace with itself. It is at one with the world around it. Cultivating your positive, befriending mind is the basic, essential spiritual practice without which all other practice falls short.

We can all cultivate a positive, befriending mind. It is a gift we can give to our family, one we can give to our friends, one we can give to our co-workers. We can give our positive, befriending mind to the entire universe. There is no greater gift.

Practice

1. When you find yourself facing any difficult or painful situation, practice asking yourself, "What deeper good might life be working toward here? What might my spirit be growing

toward through this? How can I open my mind and heart and spirit to give consent to life's purposes, however hidden they may be from my current understanding?" There is no need to come up with answers. Simply hold the questions prayerfully in your heart, resolving to remain open and accepting, with a willingness to receive insight into the deeper mysteries at work in even the most difficult circumstances.

2. Identify the major areas where you tend to become negative toward yourself, a given or recurring situation, or others. Then notice what you typically say to yourself in relationship to each area and how that solidifies and confirms your negative thoughts. How can you "reframe" what you say to yourself to be more positive, more compassionate, more hopeful and encouraging? Begin the process of reframing, redirecting your thoughts to more positive ground each time negative thoughts and feelings arise.

Reading, Day 4

BECOMING A PATIENT AND LOVING GUIDE TO YOUR OWN MIND

Like a loving and watchful parent, the sincere seeker gradually learns to guide the mind, to monitor its straying, to redirect it. The essential practice is this: to patiently and firmly turn the mind away from all illusion of negativity toward home, toward what is eternally real and ultimately true in the spirit.

Gradually, we learn: never, ever allow the mind to droop. If we do, it snowballs. It goes into a downward spiral. We need always to be alert. We need always to be awake. We need always to be open and watchful of the thoughts of the mind, observing how the mind plays, where it goes of its own accord. We need to cultivate and train our mind to become our best friend.

Most of us are not alert. We don't know or notice when the negative forces start to play. Often, it is only when we are in the abyss that we begin to realize it. Then it is very difficult to pull back, to reverse direction.

If only we could be more meditative, prayerful, in touch with our Beloved, the Beloved within! If only we could be in remembrance of the Divine within, continuously praying for the support of Divine grace, continuously praying for Divine love's protection! Then it is grace, it is love that manifests as conscious awareness of our mind.

That strength and focus of mind does not happen automatically or by accident. As human beings, we have to train our mind. So we are watchful. We are vigilant. We are keen to know what our mind is saying, where it is leading us. We do not allow our mind to become depressed, to get mired in untruth, to spin out of control, to be an undisciplined child who does not listen to us. As a good and compassionate parent to our mind in its current state of awareness, we guide it toward the best possible company. We give it the best possible counsel. We practice, practice, practice making our mind our best friend.

Steadily practicing mindfulness, prayerfulness, consciousness, our mind begins to stabilize. The intrinsic purity and luminosity of the mind begins to manifest. Remembering the unseen beneficence behind all of life's manifestations, our mind begins to glow, our mood brightens, our spirit lightens, our attunement with and delight in all of life deepens.

Channeling our thoughts from the lower to the higher, from negativity to the positive light of infinite goodness and grace, we begin to witness the most powerful miracle of all: Our mind is naturally releasing unhappiness to happiness.

Practice

1. Whenever you notice yourself falling into self-criticism, catch yourself. Befriend yourself. Remind yourself that to fall in your own self-esteem is to fall into an abyss. You are on a

journey home to your true Self, to who you are in God. The vehicle of your mind naturally veers off course from time to time. You notice when it is leaving the highway, when it is taking you on a detour by falling into negativity. You simply make an adjustment by steering your mind back to the highway of what is true.

2. If you catch yourself falling into depression, redirect your mind by recalling all of the ways grace has moved through your life. See your heart and mind being washed in light and grace until you know, again, who you are in your spirit.

3. Recall all the ways in which you serve others, the ways in which you work to give love and compassion. Affirm the beauty of your spirit as the truth of who you are. Affirm that the good in you is infinitely stronger, more powerful and enduring than any conditioned, transient, human limitation.

4. Whenever you encounter imperfection in yourself or others, remind yourself that all limitations will ultimately fall away to reveal the truth of the Divine spirit within your heart.

Bless yourself and others on their journey and cultivate compassion for all the ways in which we human beings lose our way.

5. Make it a practice to notice, to take joy and comfort in the goodness that flows through your life and every human life despite our illusory human limitations, and release all imperfections to the tender mercy and love of God for transformation.

Reading, Day 5

ATTENDING TO THE LIGHT WITHIN

There is a single web of mind, One Cosmic Mind, within which we are all living and evolving. If we are not able to be conscious of the vast Cosmic Mind, that is no problem. We do not have to worry about that. We may not know what is in the Infinite Mind, but we can become conscious and aware of what is in our own mind. We can reflect upon our own mind. We can see our own mind. We can watch our own mind rather than letting it play itself out unconsciously.

That attentive quality of consciousness, that awareness, is a kind of lamp which burns. In India, we say that temple looks best where there is a lamp continuously burning, enlightening the beautiful face of the Lord. We never allow that lamp to be extinguished.

We need the lamp in the temple, but we also need the lamp that burns ceaselessly within us. The temple priest must be careful and watchful to see that the oil does not run out. He replenishes the oil. He trims the wick to the right length to keep the lamp burning. It takes watchfulness, alertness, to keep the lamp in the temple burning. The lamp within needs our watchful mind to tend the flame that is burning in our heart.

The lamp is the flame of our aspiration. The lamp is our yearning, our love for truth, our love for all that is good and beautiful, our love for God, our love of knowing our own Self. It is our love of knowing who we are, why we are, where we are. Every fundamental question comes to be addressed, comes to resolution, provided we try to see through the lamp in our own heart and give up borrowing the answers of others.

That is the light of awareness that we need to keep aflame in our hearts. Those who have that lamp, that awareness, ever burning in their heart never go wrong in that light. They befriend everything that comes to them. They read between the lines. They come to understand the language by which God is trying to communicate to them. Such a mind is truly devoted, dedicated, offered to the Divine. Such a mind gradually gets purified and is refined until it becomes stainless once again.

Practice

1. As part of your morning prayers, spend some time writing or thinking about your deepest aspirations and longings for the coming day. Open your heart to all of the unseen forces for good in the world to bless you in making those aspirations a reality.

2. As you go through your day, notice those moments of inspiration and insight, beauty and light, peace and joy that come to you. Open your heart a little more deeply to them. Savor each moment; appreciate, absorb, and treasure the gifts of the moment, noticing what they stir in your heart, mind and spirit.

3. Spend five to ten minutes in the evening writing about what uplifted you throughout the day. What moments of human strength, courage, or tenderness were you privileged to witness or give? What kindled the ever-burning lamp of awareness in your heart? Let your heart wash a little deeper in the grace of those gifts. Make it a practice to gather the gifts of the day, to savor them in your heart, to express your deepest gratitude for them each night before going to bed.

Reading, Day 6

AS YOU THINK, SO YOU BECOME

Your befriending state of mind will attract the positive to you. As the seers of India often say, "*Yadrishi bhavana yashya siddhir bhavati tadrishibi.*" As you think, so you become. Whatever your thought, whatever your continuous thoughts, accordingly, you become that.

Infinite possibilities, incredible gifts, the Divine presence, surround you.

No moment of your life is mundane. If you are wise, if you want to be truly happy, you will learn to dwell on your blessings. You will take delight in both the large and small miracles of your life, in the mysteries of the beauty and goodness that are always present and available to you. Whatever your struggles might be, you will learn to focus on the hidden hands of grace, the subtleties of the Divine play and where they are leading you.

Life is very simple. The best friend is one's own mind. There is no need to seek outward support. Support comes from inside. The mind that is your best friend is like a fountain that is continually flowing with vibrant, sparkling water rising from its deep, pure source.

It is in the mind that we create the quality of our life. We create our own heaven and we live in that heaven. We create our own hell and we live in that hell.

If you live in hell in this world, know that your untrained, conditioned mind has helped to create and perpetuate that hell. In unconsciousness, you have framed a hell for yourself. Only you can unframe that hell.

Your thoughts do not come by accident. They come from the accumulations of the past, reaching forward to form the present. The whole of the past goes to meet the present.

Why do we need to be prayerful always, watchful always, aware always? So we will not forget reality. Then we do not cheat ourselves or anyone else. Then, at our last moment, when there can be no cheating, at that moment when you are naked to your own self, where you cannot hide anymore, you are absolutely open to your true Self. If you have practiced cultivating your positive, befriending mind for a long time, if your mind is ever steeped in Divine love, obviously in that last moment you will have the thought of God and nothing else. Your movement will be toward God because you have been nurturing thoughts of God throughout your lifetime.

If you continuously practice negative thoughts that take you away from truth, if you practice worrying, you are basically at war with yourself. You are fighting yourself. You are draining your own energy.

If you are cursing your fate, that you had this or that bad friend, that someone has caused you suffering, you are only cursing yourself. Look up. There is no enemy outside! Your only enemy resides in you! Your only enemy is inside! That enemy is your uncontrolled state of mind.

Your enemy is your own mind in ignorance of the relationship of the mind that is individual with the mind that is universal. Your enemy is your mind that is small, without understanding of its oneness with the mind that is infinite. Such a mind cannot connect between the two, so it has a very small supply of energy. Its reference point is very small, very shallow: the ego.

Anyone can throw negative at you. Whether you accept it or not depends on your readiness. Nobody should be able to catch you unaware. You can move with awareness. You can think with awareness. You can breathe with awareness. You can see with awareness. You can respond with awareness. You can always be conscious of the inner thinker, the inner seer, the inner walker. It is a question of gradual practice. It is a question of living in a state of friendship, in a state of awareness rather than ignorance or self-forgetfulness.

You cannot escape the law of the universe: whatever you give will come back to you. If you give positive, positive comes back to you. If you give negative, negative comes back to you. It is a cycle. It is up to us to anchor ourselves in the firm conviction, in the faith that, yes, we are not going to move an inch, we are not going to budge, even a little, from our commitment and dedication to our own faith in our oneness with all that is.

Practice

1. Take a few moments several times each day to keenly observe your thoughts. Observe when things are going well. Also observe when things are going badly. What are you saying to yourself about what is happening? Notice the energy, the feelings, the attitudes, the sense of possibility or lack of possibility that your thoughts stimulate, reinforce, deepen and intensify. Notice the conclusions you draw, the actions which your pattern of thinking promotes, the responses those actions evoke from others. How does all of that combine to sustain a given direction of feeling, thinking, possibility, and response? Then ask yourself, "Is this leading me where I really want to go?"

2. To recognize a mistake and invoke the power of grace to correct it is *sadhana*, spiritual practice. Whenever you recognize you are

making a mistake, decide to change and open your heart to infinite grace. Things begin changing naturally. They happen subtly. There is no need to force the process if change is not immediately apparent. Relax and let go of the mind. Allow the mind to settle. Allow it to calm. In calmness, in self-acceptance and self-forgiveness, new understanding, new direction and insight will emerge.

Reading, Day 7

UNHAPPINESS AS A CONTRACT

Happiness and unhappiness are states of mind. They are attitudes. One who dwells in the positive field of the mind, one who looks for the light in the midst of darkness, comes to realize that it is not the external circumstances that are responsible for happiness or unhappiness. Ultimately, it is our response; it is our reaction to external circumstances, our reaction to the repetitive thoughts and emotional patterns within that create our happiness or unhappiness.

A contract involves an offer and an acceptance. Both must be present to form a contract. If one party offers and the other party refuses to accept the offered terms, no contract exists. Both sides have to agree on the same terms. Anyone can make you an offer, but you are always free to reject it.

The more you practice making your mind your best friend, the less anyone can make you unhappy unless you resolve to be unhappy. No outside circumstances, no situation can make you unhappy unless you agree, unless you sign the contract to be unhappy.

It is only by keenly observing and deeply contemplating our interactions that we realize the nature of the contract to be unhappy. We are one step up on the ladder of *sadhana,* spiritual practice, when we grasp the importance of giving up any deep-seated resentment or negative clinging of our mind now and here, the instant it arises.

You need to be certain that you understand the terms of any agreement. Take the time to be sure. Don't sign until you know that what you are agreeing to creates a bond of friendliness. The bond of friendliness comes only when you sign with full awareness, knowing that you are befriending your own mind, knowing that you are truly acting on your own behalf, on behalf of your spirit.

As you become conscious and aware of a situation that triggers you, you begin to see it through the eyes of wisdom. No life is without difficulty; every life involves hardship. As you grow in wisdom, you resolve not to react. You choose to sign a contract with friendliness. You choose to harness the energy that was pulling you down and direct it into an upward movement of understanding and compassion. The emotions that would have played riot inside you are tamed under the vigilant eyes of awareness. Negative energy is transformed into a higher frequency that lifts you up, out of the darkness, into light and love. This is spirituality in practice.

No one can escape the law of *karma*, those experiences that we must go through to grow in wisdom and to deepen the life of our soul. Your soul came into this life with an agenda, with a commitment to learn certain lessons. All of your experiences derive from your soul's intention. Relax. Now is the time to shake off any clinging to the pain involved. Dive, dive, dive within yourself to find the wisdom that will carry you through to resolution.

You have signed a new contract with life, with your eternal spirit, with the Universe, with God. It is time for you to celebrate with the Universe in its unending dance of life. If you would be happy, begin consciously blessing all who bring pain into your life. They are your true friends who humble you, who soften you, who till the soil in which you can forever bind yourself to God.

Practice

1. Resolve to give up brooding over any negative contracts of the past. Whatever happened was necessary to free your soul from ignorance, to stimulate your growth in consciousness. Now is the time to shake off any clinging to the pain that was involved. Ask yourself, what did I learn from this experience? How did it enrich my understanding of human beings and of life? What do I still need to learn in order to let go of this pain? Letting go is an opportunity to become more conscious, to find your way back to peace and joy.

2. Begin the practice of consciously blessing all who bring pain into your life. They are your true friends who drive you toward freedom, toward what is ultimately real. In blessing and releasing those that seek to harm you, you are freeing yourself of all the illusion of harm. You are claiming your true Self which is free from all harm. You can authentically bless those who seek to harm you when you welcome the experience as another gateway to your true Self.

Reading, Day 8

YOU HAVE ONLY ONE FRIEND AND NO ENEMIES

You have no friend or enemy outside of you. If you think deeply about it, you will find that you have only one friend and no enemies. If you feel there is an enemy, take care of it. You take care of it by being positively oriented within your own mind. Continuous prayer, continuous meditation, continuous dwelling with those higher thoughts will gradually release the potential Divine powers within you. That gradually elevates you to a plane where negativity cannot reach you.

Positive power is within us. Negative power is within us. What we accept is up to us. There is no satisfaction in finding anybody else responsible for the miseries of our lives. That only increases the burden of our misery.

You have come to this body with the accumulated *karma* of your past lives. You have come to this life to work out a backlog of learning and unlearning. Do not add any more than what is to be burned away in this life. It is not intelligent to add to it with further negativity.

The more you resist and react to what has come to you, the more it persists, the more it lingers, the more it increases.

In India, the story is told of a cycle thief who once stood before the judge to receive his punishment. The judge asked the thief, "Did you steal the cycle?" The thief replied, "No sir, I did not." The judge said, "Pay 10 rupees and go." The thief further pleaded, "Sir, I am a very poor man. I can't afford a penny. How can I pay 10 rupees?" The judge said, "Pay 20 rupees and go." The thief continued to insist that he be allowed to go without any penalty. The judge replied, "Pay 50 rupees and go." The thief pleaded, "Sir, I will die. I can never pay that. Please forgive me." The judge said calmly and resolutely, "Pay 100 rupees and go!" The thief finally had to pay 100 rupees to be free.

This is a story about our destiny, created by none but ourselves in ignorance.

When you can be released by paying only 10 rupees, why pay 100? Everything that happens on the mental or physical plane happens due to our past karmic debts. If we pay our debts without grumbling, without further negativity, they are soon cleared.

Witness the inevitabilities of life as they come and go. Don't grumble over them. Allow the clouds to pass away, with your mind fixed on the sun of awareness of grace and light. Allow grace to work on any negative forces. Then, you find life is full of ease. You allow God to take care of you. You allow your godly mind to take care of you. You allow your Divine potential to take care of you. Thus, you have your best friend along with you everywhere you go in the world.

In such state of mind you are a renunciate monk. You may be wearing any clothes of your choice, but your state of mind is the mind of a true monk, never reactive, ever responsive. Your true seeker's mind is dwelling on the plane of that positive, one-pointed thought of the Divine potential that is within, on grace and its manifestations, on integrating and learning the subtler, deeper lessons of every life experience. Then continuously, acceptance happens. It happens spontaneously.

That is what we all are seeking in life. It is the one thing we need to achieve. It is important that we always return to a positive frame of mind. Never look through the glasses of negativity longer than it takes you to realize it. Never analyze anything from a negative frame. See the hands of the Divine behind every small instance in your life, however bitter or sweet. Convert any situation into your favor by changing your attitude toward it.

Practice

1. Morning and evening are very important transition times in which you are moving from one state of consciousness to another. Then the doors of the subconscious are more open than at any other time. This offers you an opportunity to reprogram your subconscious

mind. Completely relax your body before you fall asleep. Watch your breath and impregnate your subconscious with beautiful thoughts. Gradually your subconscious will accept them and translate them into reality in your life, blessing you with abundance and a harmoniously happy life.

2. Before falling asleep at night, affirm: I am a child of Immortal Bliss and Peace. All *karma*, all limitation, is being burned in the fire of my Illumined Mind. A foundation of joy is springing forth from within me to flood my body and mind and to spill out into the world. I live in celebration with all Creation. I am at rest in Mother Nature.

3. When you awaken each morning, take some time to be conscious that you are starting a new day. Greet the morning with a smile. Tell yourself: I am blessed to awaken to this beautiful morning, which is fresh and new. It brings new possibilities to my life. I welcome the freshness this morning brings to my body and mind, to my heart. I am grateful to Mother Nature for healing me, for renewing and releasing all that is old in my body and mind as I slept. I am healthy. Success and abundant

good will come to me as I move through the day anchored in the joy of my spirit. My joy will touch everyone I meet. I am at peace in body, mind, and spirit. All is well.

Reading, Day 9

PRACTICING PRAYER AND COMPASSION FOR OTHERS WHO ARE NEGATIVE

The more we focus on any situation with a positive, compassionate attitude, the brighter the light of our inner temple becomes. Darkness flees. The more anyone attacks us with negativity, the greater our opportunity to grow in awareness and consciousness. If we fill a person who has hurt us with the positive vibrations of our heart, with compassion and love, if we fill our own heart with prayers for that person and for our own limitations in forgiveness, compassion, and understanding, we cannot help but become healthier, happier, and more secure. We have a wider range of inner resources and a clearer mind with which to respond to the difficulty.

Compassion has to blossom in the heart. Compassion is a Divine energy, an energy of the soul. Whenever you send the positive vibrations of compassion and love to another, you are not only being generous to that person. You are first and foremost being generous and charitable to yourself because, when compassion blossoms, it brings its most powerful blessings to the heart in which it is born. The sweet energies of the soul wash your heart; they fill your mind, renewing and intensifying the life of your spirit. It is only then that compassion creates a flow, pouring those energies out to the other person.

Anyone who is behaving badly toward you is utterly miserable within. Their behavior has little to do with you. The problem is their own disturbed state of mind. To cultivate compassion, you begin opening your heart to see and feel more deeply the intense emotional and mental constrictions that afflict such a person. You authentically begin to feel toward them as you do toward a child who has made a mistake.

We support a person who is physically disabled. Our heart melts, our heart aches, for anyone who is mentally retarded or disabled. We need just as much compassion for anyone in a negative frame of mind. We might know fully well that a person is negative. As a conscious human being, however, we will not further bombard or burden that person with any negative thoughts or energy from us. As a good human being, we know that everyone has good in them if we look a little deeper, so we reinforce that good.

When we add to the negative burden anyone carries, we are damaging that person. We are damaging the whole environment. We are polluting the environment and we will be condemned to the consequences of that. We will pay a price for it, for we are a part of the pollution of the planet.

If we are truly conscious, we pray for those around us who are negative rather than condemning them. We bless them rather than obsessing on a desire for revenge, or getting stuck in any wound we feel they caused us. We uplift ourselves, we uplift them, we uplift the world with our sincere prayers for their healing and our own, whatever wrong we may feel has been done to us.

This is a very important spiritual practice because, in fact, no wrong has been done to us. We have simply paid an unpleasant *karmic* debt and we have been offered a spiritual opportunity in the process. Whenever we offer our human suffering to God and find the blessing in it, we have moved along in our spiritual journey. We are one step closer to union with God and we have brought the world one step closer to that day when others will do the same. There can be no grief in that, no regret in that. There is only cause for joy in the triumph of the spirit over this little bit of darkness that God has seen fit to give us to wrestle with and transform.

Practice

1. Whenever you feel injured or wounded by another and you find yourself brooding over how wronged you feel and their fault in the matter, turn your mind to prayer. See yourself, the other person, and the situation held in a

field of Divine light. See light flowing into your heart and mind, into their heart and mind, to resolve the situation in perfect time. Ask that the mind and heart of everyone involved be illuminated; ask for the ability to find the highest ground possible from which to view the situation.

2. If there is anyone in your life whom you feel has caused you pain and frustration or toward whom you feel deep resentment, practice this visualization:

Focus on your breath until your mind becomes calm and your body relaxed. Invite the person to appear in your mind's eye. Visualize a golden light pouring into the body of that person. See the person's face soften and light up with a smile. Fill the person with love and the positive vibrations of your mind and heart. See the person moving toward you, touched by the grace of your love and forgiveness. Embrace the person in the light of joy, in the union of your eternal spirits. Tell him or her that there is no misunderstanding or resentment in your heart, that all the past has been released.

Allow that person to gradually move into the light. You are releasing him or her into Cosmic light. See the eyes of the person fill with joy at your relationship being re-established in the subtle world of the spirit.

This will manifest in the physical level if you keep practicing this release until you achieve a relationship of harmony, peace, and joy.

3. After meditation or before you fall asleep, see and feel the light and love of your heart expanding, pouring out to all those who are afflicted around the world, sending them comfort, reassurance, inspiration, and healing.

Reading, Day 10

OVERCOMING THE FIVE AFFLICTIONS OF THE MIND

The whole purpose of the spiritual journey and of spiritual discipline is to return our mind to its stainless, innocent, pristine state of pure consciousness. All enlightened masters tell us, "You have no problem other than your impure mind." It is only in the clouded state of impurity that you lose your true vision.

Our human vision is clouded by the five afflictions of mind described by the great, ancient scientist of life, Rishi Patanjali, in his teachings on the eight-fold Yogic Path to Self Realization.

The five afflictions are *avidya* (ignorance), *ashmita* (ego), raga (attachment), *dwesha* (repulsion or aversion), and *avinivesh* (compulsive attachment to life and the consequent fear of death). Understanding these afflictions can create tremendous power of insight into the mysteries of life and the art of living.

All human beings are affected by the five afflictions of mind, which are the cause of all miseries on this planet. Human misery occurs when we allow our minds to droop, to go into negative fields, unaware. In our unconsciousness, we are unable to catch the mind when it is about to droop. In a person who is not aware, who is not conscious, who is not alert, and whose lamp is not burning, ignorance takes root in the mind. Ego manifests itself. There is attachment, repulsion, and, in the extreme case, an intense fear of death.

The first affliction of the mind is ignorance. Ignorance is a state of self-forgetfulness that is born of our naturally distorted, material perception. In ignorance, we see and accept the unreal as real and the real as unreal. It is the typical human way of seeing and relating to the physical world around us.

Our perception of the physical comes to dominate, to overpower and override our awareness of the subtler, spiritual dimensions of existence and consciousness. We forget who we are. We forget that we are a spiritual being living in a human body to refine our soul through a human experience.

In our forgetfulness, we lose access to our spiritual being, to our spiritual Self. Instead, we become attached to and identified with our body, our mind, our emotions, and our intellect. Our mind becomes clouded. Whenever we are unaware, whenever we are unconscious, we enter the state of ignorance. In that state of mind, we cannot penetrate below the skin in our perception or understanding. The pain of the body is ours, the agony of the mind is ours. We cannot separate or distinguish our Self from our experience.

There is an ancient story in India of King Janak, who called multitudes of sages and saints to his court. He wanted to have the supreme knowledge of the Self, to learn the wisdom of God from those who were wise in his kingdom. The court was open and conversations were underway when suddenly Astavakra, the great sage of that time, entered.

Astavakra's body was that of a cartoon figure, bent in eight places. He looked very strange, so everyone laughed loudly when he entered.

When Astavakra laughed louder than all the others, the court fell into stunned silence. King Janaka immediately invited Astavakra to sit on his king's seat. Janaka washed Astavakra's feet and said, "Master, I have a question. I can understand why all of these people are laughing, but I don't understand why you are laughing louder than anyone else."

Astavakra answered, "Janak, I thought you were an intelligent person. I never knew that you were a fool." Janak responded, "Why do you call me a fool? What wrong have I done?" Astavakra replied, "You have invited mere cobblers to your court in order to learn the highest wisdom of God from them. They are worthy to take care only of shoes."

When the saintly king asked him to elaborate, Astavakra responded, "Those who can only see the skin, those whose vision is only skin deep, how could they ever see the spirit within, the essence within, the Self within, the God within, the pure Mind within? Obviously, I can't take them to be wise. I was laughing to think that you have invited all of these people to give you the supreme knowledge of the Self."

Like that of the cobblers of King Janak's court, most of our knowledge is only skin deep. We cannot see beyond the superficial, the first, external layer of our experience. In ignorance, we become so deeply identified with the superficial, with our body and our untrained mind, that we come to think our body or the mind is who we are. We start accepting that which is false as true. We start accepting that which is unreal as real.

The second affliction of the mind that Patajanli defined for us is the ego. Ego is born out of, and has its foundation in, ignorance. It is a limited construct of the mind. The ego is the particular individual self that the mind has come to consider itself to be. The ego identifies and defines us; it identifies and defines our capacities. It interprets our life experience through those identifications and definitions. It falsely defines the very nature of our life, who we are, what we are capable of, all based on the distorted perceptions of ignorance.

Ego is the conditioned state of your mind and emotions in which you identify yourself with your false existence. It is the shadow of your real existence, the shadow of the real Self. Through the ego, you process your life experience, you judge others and yourself with the yardstick of your shallow perception, with the distorted and narrow, false identifications of your conditioned mind.

Through the spectacles of the false ego, we see everything as it *appears*, never the reality.

Practice

1. Compassionately observe the ways in which you identify with your limitations, the ways in which you feel defined by your failures and successes.

2. Notice what you say to yourself inwardly about your faults and counter every false statement with a true one. Find your own words, your own wisdom, the core truths which can re-establish you in the energy and possibilities of your soul. (Some examples: "This may be an old and stubborn pattern, but

it is nothing in comparison to the power of grace to transform it." "This problem is not my enemy. It is an occasion for grace, a friend of my soul that offers me the chance to grow in awareness and draw closer than ever to the wisdom of the true Self.")

3. Take time in your daily prayers to sit quietly, holding any patterns you seek to overcome up to the light of mercy and love. Trust in your will power, in concert with the Divine Will, to set anything right in your life. Rest in the certainty that the process of true transformation has begun.

4. Become more aware of those things, relationships, and activities of life which bring you the greatest pleasure and happiness. Notice what happens when they are lost to you. Step a little farther back to witness the comings and goings of pleasure and pain in your life and to accept them within the larger context of life's inevitable ebbs and flows. Tell yourself that all is well, that pleasure comes and pleasure goes, that pain comes and pain goes. Affirm your willingness to find contentment, even in the midst of those comings and goings.

Reading, Day 11

TRANSFORMING WORDLY ATTACHMENTS

Invariably the depth of worldly attraction and attachment takes deep root in the subconscious layers of the mind. Each of us develops our own preferences and priorities. When those preferences and priorities are violated, violence can erupt at any moment.

Attachment, *the third affliction of the mind,* can be external or internal. The attachment to certain people, to certain situations, outcomes, and objects, of course, is external. It can also be internal, the inner attachment to certain thoughts, concepts, ideas, philosophies, and ideologies.

Attachment conditions your mind. It grips your mind tightly. It is difficult to get away from its clutch. You cling to your concepts, your ideas. Your thoughts become a condition, a film on your mind. This thick cloud never allows the mind to see with its natural brilliance. The mind cannot shine as a clear, clean space that is without contamination or coloration.

Your ego is the foundation of attachment, the basis of all worldliness. If you feed your attachments, you multiply them without knowing it. That which you desire causes things to happen. The universe has its own sublime teaching methods.

Whatever you are attached to, that is the place from which the blows of your life will come. We are all enrolled in the university of life. Whether we realize it or not, we are constantly being groomed. We are being taught at every moment. The instant we get caught up in worldly attachments, the moment we cling to something, we attach our own concepts, our ideas, our thoughts, our philosophies to it. We won't be shaken from it. That clinging immediately results in a miserable state of mind. It is a negative force. With a force akin to gravity, it instantly begins to attract blows from outside. Then we have our lesson.

Material attachment, however, is a stepping-stone to higher levels of consciousness. It prepares the ground for a higher life, the life of Divine attachment. If you have not realized the futility, the fragility and the pain involved in materialistic attachments, you do not graduate to the higher realms of Divine love. Divine love is the unconditional love which is the foundation of the universe. It alone paves the way for true freedom from all forms of bondage and agony.

God wants our love. The universe longs for it. Until attachment is transmuted into Divine ecstasy, you can never be free.

Where there is attachment, its opposite, *the fourth affliction of the mind,* is also present: rejection and repulsion. If you are attached to something, you are inevitably going to receive a blow in relation to it. That is a given. Then you are going to be filled with that irritable state of your mind which rejects and is repulsed. You reject the blow. You object to and are repulsed by all that is counter to that to which you have become identified and attached.

Attraction and repulsion are bi-polar manifestations of the mind. They continuously pull us back and forth, from one side to the other, like a pendulum. We all swing between the two extremes of these manifestations. Go through the book of your own life to see the truth of this. The source of your greatest happiness has also been the source of your deepest insecurity and unhappiness.

When the mind is allowed to play of its own accord between these fields, we are not conscious. The mind becomes unsteady, control becomes difficult. Without proper training, anything that happens to us can rob our mind of its higher properties and the stable state of equanimity. If we allow the intensifying energies of the mind in attachment and the lower, debasing energies of the mind to play freely, havoc rules.

In our childhood days, we played with certain toys. We were attracted to them. We were attached to our toys. The time ultimately comes, however, when we throw all attachments away, like the toys of childhood.

We no longer need them. The attachment has disappeared. We no longer have the mind for them because we have grown toward something else, something more appropriate to where we are today.

The need is to practice living in a state of God consciousness rather than ego consciousness. We need to practice living in a state of Divine love rather than mere attachment to the physical or superficial. We need to practice living in the state of love and compassion rather than hatred toward others. Without love and devotion, no spiritual practice can find fulfilment. Of particular importance is being conscious of not nurturing any ill-feeling toward any member of your own family, however negative someone might be.

Practice

1. Kindly and keenly observe how attachment manifests in your life: What upsets you? What makes you anxious? When do you behave other than in ways you aspire to? Ask yourself

what attachments and expectations underlie your upsets and behaviors.

2. Notice how you are being affected by your attachments. How are others affected by them? What tolerance and resignation, what unconsciousness, what misery has accumulated in your life as a result of your attachments? What can you say to yourself to release a given attachment when it begins to arise and grip you?

3. Sit quietly, holding your most troublesome attachments in the light of mercy and love, wisdom and compassion. Ask the Divine consciousness to help you see the path to liberation, to help you develop ever deeper devotion and conscious commitment to your spirit.

4. Cultivate conscious awareness of the play between the opposite poles of attraction and aversion in your life. Become the impartial witness to this fundamental play of your mind. This will help prepare you to release attachments and avoid repulsions and aversions.

5. Practice releasing whatever attachment, aversion, or repulsion arises as you go about your day. Over time, your expanded awareness will make it difficult for the thieves of the lower mind to break into your house and rob you of the treasures of peace and harmony.

Reading, Day 12

OVERCOMING FEAR OF DEATH

The fifth affliction of the mind according to Patanjali is too much desire for life; too much clinging to life; too much attachment to the body, its senses, and all that the senses give. Out of this comes a tremendous fear of death.

Some people are haunted by the fear of death. Out of that fear comes a jungle state, a chaotic state of mind. They fall into depression.

To be positively conscious is simple. It is to be positively aware that everything that happens in our life happens for a purpose. Nothing can happen out of sheer coincidence. Nothing is an accident. What happens has to happen. There is a purpose. We discover the purpose by practicing the art of reading between the lines. We can only read between the lines with eyes that are wide open. Our eyes are not just physical eyes. We cultivate awareness, the eyes of higher levels of thought, vibration, and watchfulness.

Such persons grow in awareness and consciousness. They move to higher planes where no negativity can touch them, where no attachment can possess them, where no ego can overpower them. Ignorance is driven away because they have the lamp of awareness ever burning in their heart, enlightening the mind. Now, the mind sees through the light of God.

By awareness, we mean the light of God. These particular, small eyes of the individual are no longer the ones that are seeing. The positive, befriending mind that is our best friend is seeing. When you see through a friend's eyes, everything is friendly and good.

When we start worshipping the Divine and opening our heart in prayer, we begin to continuously expand. In that expansion, all of the constrictions, all of the narrow energy within us, and all of the consciousness begins to move, to flow. We are working to open the floodgates, to allow our conscious connection to the Divine to happen spontaneously.

Those who are blessed with a positive state of mind, those who are doing *sadhana* to attain a positive state of mind, can do and undo things by sheer will. They can do great things in this world. With their positive power of mind, they can influence any number of minds because they have befriended their own mind and made their mind their best friend.

So the most important task in life, the greatest achievement, is to seek the true friend. Our best friend is our positive state of mind. Our worst enemy is our negative state of mind. The choice is ours. These words of wisdom are given to us by those who have practiced it as the way of peace and happiness. We also are given the choice. We choose. It is up to us. Do we choose the friend, or do we choose the enemy? There is no use in condemning anyone else, for if you condemn, you shall be condemned.

Practice

1. While sitting in meditation, see yourself encircled by the light from which all creation arises. Know that light is always nourishing you, protecting you, guiding you, informing you, lifting you. See that light forming a protective shield around you as you move through the coming day. Surrender any negative that comes to you, any negative that arises within you, into that light to be burned away.

2. Affirm that you belong to the flow of infinite life. You are held in an eternal circle of creative energy and light. Remind yourself often that you walk in a universe where love is the sustaining force, where beauty is all around you. Your life arises and flows in those currents of infinite energy and creativity.

3. Affirm again and again your willingness to learn from each life experience, to gain the full measure of its contribution to your soul's consciousness and your spontaneous evolution.

4. Any time you find yourself bombarded with negative from within or without, simply step back into your heart. In your mind's eye, see yourself surrounded by a circle of Divine light. Know that light will lead you to true understanding. Notice any inspirations that come to you as you re-enter normal consciousness, then follow through with them.

5. Resolve to redirect every negative thought by holding it and the situation that gives rise to it in the light. Be assured, it is your connection with Divine light and love that will take care of all negativity. You will be in the body, free of fear, celebrating the present moment.

Reading, Day 13

PRACTICING DETACHMENT: OFFERING ALL OUTCOMES TO THE DIVINE

How do we gain release from the stubborn grip of attachment?

We begin with keen awareness of the anxiety, the misery that our attachment causes, not only to ourselves, but to those around us, to those we love. We begin to see how all attachment robs us of peace of mind. Then we begin to understand the importance of letting go. We begin to practice letting go.

The instant we realize we are in attachment to a certain outcome, we let go of our demand that life fit our limited expectations. We let go of our demand for a certain outcome. Every time we begin the day, every time we begin a new activity, we humbly dedicate it to God. We lovingly release the outcome to life's higher purposes. We open our hearts to grace, willing to become the instrument of those purposes. We simply do what we do as a servant, as a prayer, in self-offering. We do what we do for its own sake, utterly surrendering the outcome to life and to God.

A beautiful story is told of Buddha and Ananda. They were traveling together. Suddenly Buddha said, "I am thirsty. I want a little water to drink." Ananda remembered that when they were coming through the village they saw a small stream. So Ananda thought, "Let me go there for some water." He ran to the stream but, just as he got there, a bullock cart passed through the water. The water was very muddy. Ananda was in a hurry because he had to get water for the Lord. He started trying to clear the water as best he could, but he couldn't do anything. He struggled, but he couldn't find any water that was drinkable. Finally, he ran back to Lord Buddha and said, "I'm so sorry. I couldn't get you water." Buddha asked, "What happened, Ananda?

Why couldn't you get water? We saw a stream right over there; it's right over there." Ananda said, "I found the water but it was very muddy and when I tried to make it cleaner, I couldn't." Buddha said, "Ananda, go back to that place now and get me water." Ananda ran back to that place and found crystal clear water. All the dust, all the mud by then had naturally settled.

For most of us, what we try to do is from our ego. It is our vanity. We struggle to make life fit into the expectation, into the understanding that has grown in us over years of practice. We always try to set things right our way. We are like Ananda, trying to get drinkable water by frantically stirring the water. We remain thirsty; we can't have water that is clean.

Thus, it often happens when negative comes to you that, if you try too hard to fix it, if you force the situation, things only get worse. You try to manage things and nothing you do helps. At that point the best thing is to distance yourself a little, to witness the whole situation with a deep sense of trust in the

Divine design. Just let go, without muddling with it.

If you let go, if you give the outcome to God and trust, there is time. Let time settle it. Time is the healer. We need to accept the heavenly energy which is always available, which can take care of all our problems, provided we learn the art of letting go, provided we surrender our doubt, and give the outcome to God.

Trust and patience are very important to the day-to-day management of our life. Trust in Divine Providence. Trust in the Divine Mother. Trust in the wonderful intelligence of the Cosmic Process. Then have patience. If we want something to heal, we need to allow some time.

Each attachment, every expectation, is a seed that you sow to reap future unhappiness. There is such beauty in the Divine design. At certain times, sometimes in short intervals, you will be given shock treatments to help you understand that it is not good to expect. The design is continuously operating. You keep expecting that there should be no problems. Eventually, though, you find that you start contemplating, "Should I expect anything at all? Shouldn't I just let go?"

After all, you are seeking happiness and peace. You are not seeking anything else. Whatever may be the activity, whatever may be the thought, you are seeking happiness and joy and peace, nothing else. You find expectations have been leading you to misery and unhappiness. The time comes when you take stock of the whole thing, even if you don't read books and don't attend meditation classes. That doesn't matter because you are in the meditation class of the Universe. Mother Nature will teach you. She teaches everybody. We create miseries with our expectations. Eventually, we learn. It is only when we expect nothing, when we offer ourselves and all outcomes to God, that we are flooded with peace and joy.

Practice

1. Whenever you are moving from one activity to another, make it a practice to pause. First, be grateful for what you have just

completed and everything you learned from it. Then offer all of your efforts, the results and outcomes of what you are about to undertake, to the Divine.

2. As you begin a new activity, open your heart and still your mind, if only for a few seconds, to receive the nameless energies of Divine grace, inspiration and guidance. You are just receiving now. You are creating space in your heart and mind for Divine energy and creativity to move ahead of you, to form and express life's intention through this upcoming activity. Release all the outcomes to whatever your Higher Power is and begin. Observe how you receive the guidance and inspiration you need to respond to each moment as it unfolds.

3. As you start to work on any project, consciously hold your heart open to the higher purposes of life and to any unknown and unanticipated ways that you can serve life and others through your work. Notice the unexpected miracles, large and small, that come from that openness.

Reading, Day 14

KEEPING COMPANY WITH THE POSITIVE

It is natural to be fearful. It is more natural to conquer fear. In truth, by nature, you are fearless.

Positive thoughts, courage, and continuous affirmations that make your path to peace of mind and Self-Realization easier are your best friends. You need to keep company with them always. That is the Holy Company that is already within your heart. Avoid the unholy company of the negativity of your mind. If you are in the company of the Holy One, the positive One, you will glow. You will be happy. You will be graceful. You will be full of life. You will celebrate every moment because you are alive. You are no longer the living dead. You are alive moment to moment, in awareness.

Life, by design, is a continual process of self-discovery. The more harmonious we become in our living, the more we bridge the gap between our thoughts inside and the world outside. We become more alert and conscious. We don't easily surrender to negative thoughts, to negative brooding, or to any negative bombardment from outside. We watch and pause; then we move as a true friend of the spirit.

All beings on earth and in the myriad universes are eternally connected to the Divine source. Each plant, each animal, each natural element, each human being, is a sublime manifestation of Divine life, an exquisite incarnation of Divine beauty and love, an embodiment of Divine nature. Study this in your heart and in your experience. The world around you is a living revelation.

Your life and all life around you is the loving touch of the living body of God. Even the harshest and most fearsome manifestations of human life are sources of revelation. They teach us, however painfully, of the terrible and deadly cost of forgetting that our true life is rooted in and devoted to the Divine.

The Divine is within. It is forever singing through the world around us. Our task is to awaken to it until we see it everywhere, until we hear and feel it in every moment: in every aspect of the creation we encounter and the life we are given. As a sincere seeker of the spirit, we train our mind, we attune our heart to the Divine at play within and around us. We contemplate these truths until we feel the Divine singing through the world and our own being, always.

Practice

1. Practice becoming watchful and alert so you can understand when your mind is going in the wrong direction. At that point, catch yourself. Say to yourself, "My child, this is no way to behave. You are my best friend. How could you talk like this? You are talking like an enemy. No. You are my best friend." Then embrace your mind with all love, with all compassion. Find a way to lead your mind with

thoughts of higher vibration, with thoughts of higher light, with the wisdom of the sages and saints who have illumined the path of reality for you.

2. In moments of leisure, take yourself to some place of tranquility where nature surrounds you, where there are open spaces, trees, or beautiful flowers. Commune with the energy and beauty there. Contemplate the rhythms of life around you. Open your body and mind to the rich, subtle harmonies of the natural world that gave birth to you. Let those harmonies speak to you, inform you, lead you deeper into the peaceful harmonies of your own spirit.

Reading, Day 15

BLESS ALL, HARM NONE WITH YOUR WORDS

The gift of speech is so commonplace to human beings that we fail to appreciate the true magnitude of its power to bless or to harm. Words have incredible power. That power, how we can use it to bless ourselves and others, how we misuse it to hurt ourselves and others, and the thoughtless habits we fall into with regard to it, offer us an immense resource for cultivating mindfulness.

We are all insensitive from time to time. We lash out in anger. We gossip. We fall into teasing without realizing the personal cost to the one on the receiving end of our humor. We can be oblivious to the threshold at which a joke becomes ridicule. We need to take care, when we are speaking, that we are not doing so at the expense of any other human being.

In a group, we often derive enjoyment at the cost of others. We talk easily of others' faults and weaknesses, often simply because we don't know how else to keep a conversation going. We find endless and myriad ways to put others down — in order to elevate ourselves in our own mind or in the minds of others — all without grasping the damage we are doing to ourselves and to those about whom we speak so harshly.

Without conscious awareness, words can be hurtful. We realize it too late, after the damage is done, when the words cannot be taken back. Then, any effort we make to correct our mistake often only makes the situation markedly worse.

We forget that our view is distorted. We cannot see anything as it is. We have a pathetically limited frame of reference. When we are judgmental, we are like a strainer finding fault with a hole. We search for the faults in others while overlooking our own imperfections.

Our judgmental thoughts and comments create difficult situations. They send negative energies into the world that replicate and multiply their own virulent essence. Ultimately, they bring that essence back to us. Be mindful of any act that hurts others. One day we must pay for every harm we do.

When we repeat harmful acts, they gradually become second nature to us. Their negative, discordant energies accumulate in our hearts and minds. They store themselves in our bodies, creating discomfort and disease. They multiply the possibilities for our personal disgrace and for harm to come to us.

Kind and loving words can bridge all differences. They create the foundations of peace and harmony in all relationships.

There are those who are true gifts to humankind. Their words are charged with positive energies that uplift and strengthen the human heart and soul. We are rejuvenated in their presence. If for some reason they have to criticize, they do so with empathy, using constructive, encouraging and compassionate words. The other person never feels put down.

The world has enough venom. There is a plethora of negatively minded people in every society. Don't join the herd. Stand up boldly. Speak in harmony with the path of enlightenment. By respecting others, you respect yourself. By uplifting others, you uplift yourself.

Give by being a good listener as well. When you learn to listen to the other's point of view with a non-judgmental mind, you hear beyond words. You feel and see who is speaking behind the words. From that place, the appropriate words come naturally to soothe and heal the wounds of others.

Be a healer. When your mind is filled with love and compassion, your heart will overflow with the urge to bless and heal others. Then all who meet you will be blessed. The pure mind is a pure blessing for all humankind. Pure mind sees the good, the Divine spark, in everyone. It sees the purity and perfection in everything!

Practice

1. Think about the power of language and the way you personally use it to bless and to harm. Take the vow to bless all and hurt none!

2. Cultivate greater awareness of how you use language. Become attentive to the quality of your speaking. What does it reveal about who you are being in this moment? What does it contribute to others? Where is this conversation coming from, where is it leading, at an energetic level? How can you redirect it when necessary?

3. If you find yourself engaged in a negative conversation, remember your commitment to bless rather than harm. If necessary, openly admit you feel uncomfortable with being so negative and explore with the other person how you both can redirect the conversation.

4. If you find yourself in an angry, accusatory exchange, simply admit that this is not constructive for anyone and take a break. Search your soul for the capacity to accept and understand. Don't come back to it until you

can be compassionate and constructive, until you can bless the other person with what you have to say and hear their side of the issue.

Reading Day 16

ARISE, AWAKE, ACCEPT: THREE CORNERSTONES OF SPIRITUAL PRACTICE

If you do not arise into your spiritual inheritance, if you do not awaken to your own mind and lift it into the light of higher truth, if you do not accept all that life brings you as the gift that it is, no amount of prayer, meditation, or spiritual practice will make a difference. You may sit before God. You may pray and meditate. You may perform other spiritual practices, but you will remain asleep.

"Arise! Awake! Accept!" are the three cornerstones of spiritual practice. They are essential. Until you embrace them as central, you cannot be other than subject to the whims and vagaries of your untrained mind.

Work the soil of your own mind. The more you do so, the more confident you become in life and in your mind. You move away from fear and doubt.

If you leave your mind to its own upward and downward cycles, the downward cycles gradually dominate. Gravity overtakes you. You feel more and more defeated. Fear and doubt and guilt begin to grip you. They live like parasites in your body and mind, sucking your life energy, sucking your life's potential, sucking life itself away.

You sleep for six to eight hours. For the remainder of your day, you only think that you are awake. The typical waking state, however, does not even approach wakefulness. Most of us remain deeply asleep. We eat, we talk, we see and respond to the people, the circumstances, and the world around us in the dull and dim awareness of habit. We live unconsciously, existing within the limits of what we believe we already know. We are sleepwalkers.

The greatest challenge any of us faces in life is to wake up, to awaken from the sleep of unawareness into the vibrancy and joy of pure awareness. The practice of awakening to the deeper, truer, more expansive realities within each moment and making the ancient wisdom of the Great Ones our own is essential to being human. Magnificent, subtle and uplifting dimensions of existence lie beyond the physical, beyond our current levels of awareness, beyond our current assumptions and beliefs. They are the healing, unifying leaven of life, a leaven which lifts us and, through us, lifts the world. They provide the fertile ground from which more humane qualities surface and mature for our own happiness and for the happiness of others.

When we are asleep, walking in unawareness, we miss the essential, magical nature and qualities of our Being within and of life itself. We never come to know our true Self, the one who is constant, the one who experiences. We never come to know true, enduring joy. We never come to know the deep pervading sweetness of life itself. We live superficially, caught up in the external, in the excitement, struggle, or diversion of the moment. Any occasional happiness is inevitably followed by unhappiness. We miss life's promise, what could be, what is meant to be.

Awaken your consciousness. Arise to claim the magnitude of your true inheritance. Until you awaken, you are vegetating, confined to your personal struggles and concerns. A larger life awaits you. Life is expansive. Spirit is expansive. You are expansive in your nature.

As you awaken and arise in the higher, unifying life of your spirit, you accept. You accept everyone you meet as a spiritual being like yourself. Confronting your own limitations with compassion, you become more appreciative of the problems and weaknesses of others. You stop focusing on the material faults and ignorance of others. Anger and resentment toward those who cause you pain diminishes. You no longer fight against anyone else as "the enemy." The pain of others affects you as much as your own. Your concern for the less privileged deepens. As your spirit grows in understanding, you no longer fight against what comes to you. You perceive the sustaining grace available to you in all of your experience. You learn to trust, to accept where life is leading you.

As you continue to practice wakefulness, you accept the truth that grace alone is all-powerful. You surrender ever more deeply to the love and protection of the Divine as the simple way to peace. This is the path of your heart. You are now ready to accept the wonders of Divine love and light.

Arise, Awake, and Accept until you reach your Home.

Practice

1. In the simple path of *bhakti*, of surrender and devotion, you are watchful and keen. When doubt comes, watch it as a fleeting thought, apply the antidote of your love, and trust in the Divine. Let your faith in God, in Life, and in Goodness give you enough confidence to rule out all doubt.

2. Tell yourself often, "You are safe. You are not alone anymore. All of the Universe loves and supports you. All is well."

3. Affirm often: "No fear, no doubt can survive in the enlightened shrine of my heart."

Repeat this practice time and time again, until those doubts which bring you so much restlessness, the ones that destroy your inner peace and your harmony with others, have stolen away in silence. This is the power of *bhakti*, the power of love for all that is Divine.

Reading, Day 17

THE PATH THROUGH YOUR HEART

Without devotion and love, no effort on your part will bear the fruit of freedom. You cannot find the infinite spirit within you without first reaching your heart. Until you come to that place of love, you have nothing. All of the Great Ones had to come to Supreme, Unconditional Love. Devotion and love are the essence, the essence of the spirit, the essence of creation, the essence of life itself.

It is in the heart that we experience and deepen our connection to others. Our ultimate relationship is with the Infinite Divine. The name by which we call it is irrelevant. It is the living Divine essence within the name that matters. The Divine is inexhaustible. It has a thousand names, a thousand faces.

We grow closer in that relationship through the good we seek and work toward in our life, through the love we give to others, through daily prayer and worship, chanting, and spiritual companionship. Our heart opens a little bit at a time. The movement is incredibly subtle.

We are like a child being carried by its mother from one room to the other. The child doesn't know the mother lifted her to move her to bed when she was asleep, but the movement has taken place. It is not always easy to perceive, it is not always easy to understand, how the Divine is moving us. Only the Divine Mother knows. The child does not know. The Divine Mother takes us from one place to the other, from one level of consciousness to the other, in a continual process, without our knowing it.

That is the reason you should never lose heart. Even if at times your mind is not settling down, don't lose heart. Your perseverance is what God wants to see in you, not what you do. God wants to see your steadfastness. Are you are ready to persevere in spite of the fact that you have not experienced anything whatsoever? Is your movement, your wish, your love, subject to certain experiences? If it is subject to certain conditions or experiences, you are putting obstacles in the path of your devotion and realization.

You will have inspirational flickers from time to time. Experiences will come to tell you, "Yes, I am listening to you. I am watching you. I know that step by step you are crawling toward me like a small child." That is what spiritual experiences are about. They encourage and inspire you to keep going through the arduous journey. They are not the journey itself, however; they are not the point of the journey.

Be childlike. With absolute innocence in your heart, offer yourself unconditionally to God.

Surrender. Embrace the ways in which you are being moved to higher ground through every experience. Everything that comes to you comes from the infinite flow of life. It is the loving hand of God's personal instruction for you. Within every experience is a call to you as the Divine Child to awaken. Make up your mind. Move through complete surrender and trust, through the heart.

What is important is your doubt-free state of mind.

Love and doubt are conflicting conditions. Love and doubt are incompatible. If you doubt someone you love, they feel hurt. If you love the Divine, if you say you love God and in spite of that you nurture doubts, you love but you doubt. Love with doubt is self-contradictory. We must recognize this inherent incompatibility.

Practice

1. We notice when we are nurturing doubts. When doubts come, we watch them. We counteract doubt by acknowledging it as a dark patch, a shadow enveloping the mind and heart. The only way to drive out darkness is with light. So we hold all sense of darkness, all shadow, all doubt, tenderly in the light, opening our heart to the illumination that God will surely send.

2. If doubt is ever present, there is another side, which is trust. You have only to say to yourself, "Yes, I have doubt in my heart. So what? I also have tremendous trust in Life, in God. This doubt is nothing. This doubt cannot stay in my mind, because the power of my trust in my Beloved is so strong. The grace and the light and the strength of all the saints, of all the Holy Ones, are always available to me, always with me. Doubt cannot stay."

3. Affirm to yourself time and again, "All negativity, all doubt, is trivial and utterly powerless when I hold myself in the light of the Holy Ones, when I cling to the feet of the Divine." Practice this whenever doubt and negativity arise. Resolutely meet all doubt by reaffirming the loving presence and grace of God.

Reading, Day 18

THE WORLD: A PLACE OF LEARNING

The soul and consciousness evolve through experience. The world is a place of continuous learning. The mind carries its impressions forward, from one day to another, from one body to another, from one birth to another. This is the journey of life that does not stop with death. Death is only a short pause between two levels of experience, gross and subtle. You leave the gross body to enter into the subtle plane of consciousness. If your consciousness is governed by earthly desires, however, you must return again to the grosser level of the body to work through those desires. You keep coming back until you learn to perceive what is real and eternal and to let go of what is unreal and transient.

Living in the world, a world of continual change, it is only natural to become identified with the body and its senses. The magnitude and quantity of gross phenomena around you tends to overpower the more subtle aspects of consciousness. Inevitably you come to experience certain difficult situations, which function like natural shock treatments. Whether you are illiterate or highly educated, rich or poor, at times you stumble over obstacles which appear insurmountable. You suffer.

There are times of annihilation, of utter devastation, in every life. No one escapes. These, too, are part of the human experience. If you learn how to respond to these obstacles, how to receive the deepest wounds of your humanity in a way that opens your heart and expands your consciousness, your spirit is revealed. You find healing. You are freed from the tyranny of circumstance. You are purified by the process.

That is what surrender is all about. If you humbly surrender, if you accept the wounds as well as the joys of life when they come, if you resolutely dive deep within to see with the eyes of the soul, wisdom is born. Compassion is born.

That is why Jesus taught, "Resist not evil." What we resist persists. We become like that which we love. We also become like that which we hate. Which will be stronger in you? Will it be your love, your compassion, your forgiveness, or your hate, your resistance?

Accept the blow of even the hardest teaching when it comes. Dive deep, deep within yourself to find that place from which you can derive peace and understanding and compassion with regard to what is happening to you. When you confront the internal or external carnage brought about by human ignorance, greed and hatred, take refuge in God, in the eternal principles. Surrender. Allow the soul to nourish you. Allow all that is not your essential being, all that is not your essential goodness, to be shaken loose in the storms of your life. Be the reed shaken in the wind for God's hidden purposes, even when they elude you. For "He who loses his life shall save it, and he who saves his life shall lose it."

The obstacles, the agonies of your life, then become entrances into the world of spirit. They are initiations into *bhakti*, into deeper devotion and compassion.

Life will not be confined to your preconceptions of what it should be. It is infinite. It is exquisite in its subtlety. It is relentless in its workings to reveal its Oneness. Let the outer shell of your illusions be shattered, so that you are no longer an instrument of the illusion which is a scourge upon the earth. Whatever you are experiencing is ultimately beneficent if you choose to discover its beneficence. Then you become a co-creator with God, gleaning every aspect of the love that God extends to you.

However much a disbeliever we might have been, most of us eventually come to believe that there is some greater power, some higher intelligence, some higher design at work. We get glimpses into other realms through our joys and sorrows. Those realities take root in the heart. Possessive, materialistic attitudes gradually lose hold. The energy level of the mind rises and we begin perceiving newly.

I met a wonderful old woman in Crestone, Colorado, one of the most highly charged spiritual places in the U.S.A. When I was talking to her, she said, "You know, I learned a lesson from this machine [from which she received oxygen]." She lived at an altitude of 8,000 feet. She didn't need extra oxygen at 300 feet in St. Louis. She said, "This machine has taught me something. Always before in my life, I thought I breathed. Now, I know I have no power, not even to breathe."

The day you come to realize that you don't even have the power and freedom to breathe, that day you truly become devoted. Not before. Before that you are only moving toward devotion.

Devotion is a commitment. It comes only through deep experience. It can't be borrowed. It doesn't come from books. If it does come, it never leaves you. The feeling that she couldn't breathe on her own never left that woman until the day she died. As long as she understood that she didn't even have the freedom to breathe, she also knew the only thing she did have was faith. She told me, "Now I have faith in God. I don't understand much. I don't read much. I have no knowledge. But, yes, I have faith." What is faith, but love and trust in God?

We have love in our heart. That is natural. We give that love to anyone, to everything in the world, but we don't give it for its own sake. In return, we want happiness. We hope everyone we trust will return us a little happiness. In so doing, in so giving, we are disappointed. We suffer. Gradually, through surrender, we learn. We finally come to see that what we were seeking was only in our imagination, our expectation. It was not reality. Only then do we seek the Ultimate Reality.

Practice

1. Practice inquiring of yourself, "What kind of true freedom do I enjoy? What pseudo-freedoms do I cling to? What kinds of bondage do I create for myself? How do I enslave myself with what I buy from the marketplace? How do I chain myself in the relationships with which I fill my time? What kinds of

attachments fetter my body, mind, intelligence, and spirit?

2. Accept the pain of your attachments rather than judging them. Allow them to lead you to that place where you can say, "No, this is too painful. It is better that I cling only to God."

Practice surrendering to God as your true resource, your only source of wealth, your only security. Cling to God through the storms of your life. Rely on God for all the comfort, love, and assurance you have been seeking elsewhere. Let go of everything else but your trust in God.

Reading, Day 19

YOUR HEART AS THE CENTER OF THE UNIVERSE

Yes, your heart is the center of the universe. It is from the heart that you expand to embrace, to offer your deepest emotions to all beings. It is that expansion of the heart that brings you the greatest fulfillment. God did not choose the head as residence. God always chooses to reside in the sacred shrine of the heart. Your head cannot be the shrine. Your heart is the shrine. That is where God lives, that is where you, the Self, live.

As you go through the pains and tribulations of life, you try to understand the simple thread that runs through your varied experiences and daily chores. You come to realize that beyond your pains and pleasures there is a higher purpose. You realize that beyond your tiny ego-self there is someone mightier than you, who takes care of the many details which you often forget, or which you cannot manage by yourself. Here comes that unseen force, that subtle presence which manifests in your feeling heart.

You begin to feel a connection. First it is a thought. Then it is a feeling, a deeper feeling, the deepest feeling from the center of your being, the heart.

It melts you, humbles you. You start feeling closeness with the Divine, whom you always thought to be far away from you, in some distant heaven.

Now, you feel the Divine presence closer to you. You open your heart in deeper intimacy, communicating, confiding, relying on your newly found Beloved. This new intimacy with the Divine helps you to release all that is necessary to become lighter and closer to your Self, to the Divine in you, to God within you.

Your heart pumps blood into your arteries and veins that breathe life into each cell. But what is blood? What is blood really bringing to your body? Blood is energy. It is joy. It is love and nourishing life. That is what the heart is pumping through your body. When your heart center is open, joy and love flow through your veins and arteries like a beautiful creek, creating celestial music of inner peace and joy. Your cells are rejuvenated, they dance with life and you are healthy, you are healed.

When your heart is closed, you feel constricted. The flow is obstructed; you feel disconnected from the world, lonely, depressed. The creek seems to be dry. It cannot flow; it cannot dance; it cannot sing.

That is what we see in any society madly running after money. When money becomes our ultimate value, our only god, it steals the power of the heart to pump joy and love. The stream of life runs dry. When the true God, the God of Love, is our focus and attention, the stream becomes alive. It starts to dance its way to the ocean of joy and love.

Your heart sees through the eyes of unity. The head divides. The heart unites. The head discriminates, tries to rule and control. The heart unifies the broken threads of life and harmonizes the discordant notes into a Divine symphony. In the heart, the master of the ceremony of life sits, conducting the ceremony of celebration and communion, unity and universality.

Your heart is your home away from home. The loving Divine Father and Mother always sit in the sacred shrine, calling you home. There is no rest until you retreat to your Source, the center, the heart. You journey home through your practice of making your mind your best friend. You feel the Oneness with everyone, with everything. You celebrate.

This is the goal of human life. You, I, all are born to attain this state. We are born to dissolve all discrimination and divisions into love, which manifests through our heart. May we all open our heart to the music of the Divine. This music is perennial. It never ceases. It is the eternal music of creation, an eternal celebration of life.

Practice

1. Practice consciously experiencing the present moment through the energies of your

heart. Allow the energies of the heart to open and pour out into all that you are doing.

2. Imagine your heart to be an open bowl sitting on the altar of all that is sacred. See and feel it receiving ineffable wisdom and guidance from all that is, from all that wants to be born through you. Get in touch with the feeling and energy of your infilling heart throughout the day.

3. Before you begin a new task, look into your heart for just a moment. Open your heart to receive all the blessings and opportunities for service and grace that are available to you through this activity. Just let the heart fill with energy and love and pour the Divine into all that you do. Know that the Divine is going ahead of you to shape your life's purposes. Then be attentive to any grace that comes that is beyond what you could have anticipated.

Reading, Day 20

WE ARE ALL SEEKERS OF ANANDA: JOY, BLISS ETERNAL

We all are radiant spirits, children of the Infinite. We are all embodiments of bliss eternal — embodiments of pure, Divine, all-encompassing love. As such, we are all seekers of *ananda*, the natural bliss of our eternal being. We all are seeking the joy of our true being. That is why we seek so relentlessly for happiness.

No one wants to be afflicted with diseases and suffering. Yet, these are part of daily life. The goal of life is to realize that we are not this fragile body, this fragile mind, this fragile intelligence that changes, dies, and decays. We are that which was never born and that which shall never die.

Our true nature is happiness. None of us wants to die because we are, in truth, deathless. The only purpose of the spiritual journey is to realize this. Everyone is afraid of the journey, nonetheless, because it treads a path unknown, uncharted, uncertain. It is unpredictable.

We have to give up our ego — who we think ourselves to be — in order to experience our infinite reality, who we really are. That is the biggest challenge. We are afraid. We are afraid that if we give up our ego, we will be non-existent; but we are no more than vegetables until we awaken to complete, childlike trust in the Divine.

What is most precious to God is our complete trust. We are all meant to have a child's trust in our Beloved, to sing to God of our love and trust with absolute abandon. When, in innocent surrender and delight, we manifest complete trust in all our actions, in all our thoughts, in all our deeds, we have a child's trust. Our husbands and wives, our mothers and fathers, our children and co-workers, our neighbors and friends will feel that one reality in our heart and all will be blessed immeasurably.

Practice

1. Meditate often on all the gifts that God has given you. Write about them often.

2. The most sublime gifts are your body and your mind. Contemplate the miracles that God unfolds through your body and mind at every moment. You cannot even breathe without God breathing through you. Contemplate the miracle of your eyes, your hands, your legs and feet, and all of the systems of your body, which work harmoniously together without your conscious attention. Fill with gratitude and your love for God for all that you have been given. You are heir to the entire universe. The kingdom of mind, which is your birthright, is designed to bring you to union with your Divine Mother and Father and with all of Creation.

3. Affirm to yourself time and again that you are the embodiment of *ananda*, joy eternal, and

that no doubt or disease can touch your spirit. In spirit, you are eternally pure and peaceful.

Reading, Day 21

THE AVAILABILITY OF GRACE

Throughout every age, God has sent saints, sages, and enlightened souls to earth to rekindle our awareness of our intimate connection to all that is Divine. The saints and masters are living beacons of the destination of our own journey. They work eternally to uplift humanity and the human spirit. They are our guides into the highest dimensions of life. Those dimensions are beyond the perception of the physical body and the physical senses. They are beyond this physical, manifested world.

All of the grace of the enlightened ones, all of their prayers and austerities, all of their spiritual practices, all of the blessings which have emanated from them are still emanating at this moment. Those vibrations, that grace, those blessings are in the ether. The sublime vibrations of all those who have been living a holy life, a life dedicated to Divinity, are always around us. All of that grace surrounds us. It permeates every atom of the Universe and is always available to each of us.

Grace is always working on a very subtle plane. Maybe many of us are not conscious of it, but it is working. It is working every time we have an intuitive glimpse; every time we have a subtler feeling; every time we are drawn into something good, toward something higher in life. Every time we have a flowering of mercy or goodness; every time good comes to us from some unknown, unseen source; every time such things happen in our life, it is, again and again, Divine grace. It is the blessings of the Holy Ones who have worked for the betterment of human consciousness throughout time.

God requires only two cents from us in exchange for life's infinite blessings. Those two cents are our offering, our *dakshina*, to life, to the infinite. *Dakshina,* in Sanskrit, is the seeker's offering to the Divine, to the teacher of the soul. The first cent is trust — trust in the eternal teachings. *Shraddha*, in Sanskrit, means trust and faith. If those who are enlightened teach that through compassion you reach higher compassion, then you need to faithfully trust and practice compassion. You need to practice forgiveness in your life. The more faithfully you practice, the more humbly you offer and surrender yourself to your practice, the deeper your trust and faith become. The truth of the teachings becomes your own. So the first thing that is very important is faith and trust. That is the first offering to the Divine that you need to give.

The second cent that we need to always offer is our patience, our perseverance. Patience in the material world pays. Patience in the spiritual world pays infinitely.

If we are not patient and persevering through all the tests and tribulations in our life, which are but blessings to us, we will not be able to reach a higher state. The greater the tribulations we face, the greater the potential for grace. We need to be prepared. We prepare by attuning our mind with trust and patience.

In family life, if you have trust between husband and wife, there is harmony and balance. If you have trust between the mother and the children, there is harmony and balance. If there is trust between superiors and junior staff, there is harmony and peace. Practicing patience and perseverance can bring you all the blessings you seek. With trust, with faith in all that is presented to you in your life, offer your love and patience and perseverance, your steadfast devotion to the highest possible good. Then move steadily forward, in harmony and balance.

Practice

1. Take a moment to open your heart to the infinite grace of the Holy Ones each morning. Affirm in your mind the truth that the self-realized masters never die. They merely give up their physical bodies, transcending time and space, to be eternally available to all of humankind. Receive the tender and countless blessings they wish to bestow on you this day.

Let the energy of those blessings fill you, body, mind, and soul.

2. Offer yourself as an instrument of Divine blessings to others. See and feel Divine love, Divine light, the incomprehensible blessings of the Holy Ones, pouring through your heart and out to all those you meet as you go through the day. Send those blessings out, to touch and uplift all other beings on earth, to heal all beings who are suffering. Become a radiant channel of blessings for all children of our Mother, the Earth.

3. Human beings are very sensitive to the energy of other human beings on the physical plane. Your prayers are powerful. Whenever you learn of some tragedy, some horror or wrong in the world, rather than becoming reactive or despondent, hold all those who are suffering in the flow of infinite healing. Invoke the love, blessings and comfort of all the Holy Ones who have ever lived to sustain and guide those affected through their difficulty.

4. Spend time outside often, meditating on the beauty of the natural world and its harmonies. Allow those harmonies to enter

you. Experience Nature as the loving mother and source of revelation that she is. Experience her harmonies, her energy, and her beauty as the womb of your existence. Her nature has formed you. Her nature is within you. Experience the wonder in that.

Reading, Day 22

LEARNING TO SEE WITH THE EYES OF THE SPIRIT

Everything in our lives is a part of the process of human evolution. Whatever we do is not only for ourselves but also for the whole of human society in its process of evolution to a higher state of consciousness. Our human experience compels us to question life, to question ourselves more deeply. That is the design of the life process.

What are we seeking? What is the source of true happiness? Is it more things? Or, is it discovering the bliss, the *ananda*, of our essential being? What leads to true peace?

These questions bring new light to the human mind. We discover the need for a different perspective, the need to learn to see beyond the physical dimension, the need to see with the eyes of the spirit.

Those who have lived the eternal principles through the ages have left us a legacy, but it is one with which we need to personally experiment. We must find out whether these principles are practice-able in our own lives, in the day-to-day struggles of our own existence. It is only through practice that we experience truth directly. It is only through practice, through our own experience, that we truly learn.

We humans, according to all the enlightened ones, can never find peace until we pause. We must withdraw from our senses. Our senses are naturally focused externally. Our energies move outward to the manifested Cosmos, in continuous interaction with the world. That outward focus on sensual pursuits creates a constant energy drain.

When we rise up, when we bring those energies together to focus them inwardly in contemplation and meditation, we discover a new, untouched dimension. We discover the wealth and treasure that lie waiting in the Holy of Holies, in the shrine of our own heart.

There God sits, the Eternal Presence, our One Beloved.

God is not sitting in silence in our hearts. God sings a song of eternal joy. In India, we call it the Song Celestial, the *Bhagavad Gita*. The Lord is not mute. He is sitting with a flute. He is calling us. He is calling us all into that world of joy, which is the shrine of our heart, the essence of our being, our own Self.

Though we seek and search outside, depending on external things to find happiness, we find true happiness only through our longing to move within. There we experience the Celestial Song Divine, the *Gita*, not as a concept, but a sweet, living reality.

Practice

1. Practice responding to the faintest stirrings of your own heart. These are the quickenings of your soul. They are the delicate and vulnerable stirrings of the new life which seeks to be born through you. Practice noticing them, listening to them, spending some time with them, following the thread of their

inspiration as the thread of your own unfolding, highest Self.

2. Retreat inward, if only for a second, when something stirs you. If necessary, go back to it during the evening. Quietly explore those feelings, those moments of inspiration of your heart, a little more fully each day. Journal about them. Let them gather in your mind and heart. Let them lead you to your deepest aspirations and longings. Let them move and flow and work through you until they become intimate friends, until they literally sing and their singing fills every cell of your body. That, too, is prayer.

These are the threads of your unfolding. Given your full, absorbent attention, they will gather in the eyes of your soul like the faint light of distant stars, until they can be seen and understood, until they can find ways to fully express themselves through you.

Reading, Day 23

ON DESTINY, FREE WILL, FREEDOM, AND GRACE

Around the world, seekers of different faiths and traditions ask if our life is predestined. The simple and truthful answer is yes, for the past has created the present and the present creates the future. Destiny continues to unfold as a matter of cause and effect. What *is*, both in our own lives and in the life of the world around us, proceeds from what has been.

This answer, however true, gives rise to an even more important question. If everything is predestined, what is the role of individual will? Do we have any freedom? This is a difficult, confounding, enduring mystery for humankind.

As long as we are ignorant of our true identity, as long as we have not found our inner existence, our Eternal Reality, our lives are predestined. Only by finding the authentic being, the true Self within, which is infinite existence, knowledge and joy, can we unravel the mystery of destiny.

We cannot borrow the answer. No philosophy can resolve this ancient riddle of human existence. The essential question, the one that must be personally answered, remains: Who am I?

The self you think yourself to be, the self with whom you have been identified, is limited. It is a pseudo-self, a limited self that is governed by the past. It is the ego, the obstacle between you and the realization of a more ultimate freedom. As long as you are in the grip of the ego's narrow illusions, you cannot be free. You are a prisoner of the past and the destiny that proceeds from it.

It is only by mastering your own mind that you escape the inevitable wheel of destiny and the confines of individuality. If you are circumscribed by individuality, you are within its operational range, whether you accept it or rail against it. Enlightenment is the transcendence of individuality through universality. To be enlightened is to recognize that all is One.

The only way to transcend the ego is to become conscious, to continually surrender your limited awareness into an ever-expanding awareness of Universal Oneness, to rely ever more deeply on the infinite, on grace.

Grace is essential. We all have individual will power. Everything that we have achieved in life has come out of our intention and will to attain. We all have the aspect of effort, our individual will to attain. Our effort combines with the grace of the Divine, which unfolds to assist us in achieving our goals. Without grace, nothing can be achieved.

With grace, all that is impossible becomes possible. All of life's obstacles become steps toward higher realization. We open our hearts to grace, and grace opens our hearts to realize the purpose of every situation presented to us. Until and unless we open to grace, we cannot transform the more difficult situations of our lives. With grace, even the most negative forces become agents for the positive, lifting us into a higher life, into higher energy, into more expansive consciousness.

Our hearts must open in acknowledgment of the infinite grace that surrounds us. It is not enough to read scripture and participate in spiritual discussions. More important is to practice opening to grace, to let grace sing in our lives, until we realize that the Celestial Song is the song of our own heart.

Practice

1. Spend a few moments consciously holding your heart open to the grace being bestowed on you and your coming activities. If you find yourself in a difficult situation during the course of the day, turn inward again to the presence of grace. Feel the energy of grace flowing through you, into the situation, into the hearts of any others involved. Let grace inform and guide you as to how to respond to the situation.

2. Ask yourself when confronted with difficulties: What conduct, what attitudes, what changes, what courses of action on my part, would be in alignment with grace? Surrender the smaller, lower, more predictable impulses

of the ego and follow through with the higher path informed by grace.

3. Cultivate awareness of and offer gratitude for the magnitude and availability of grace and the difference it makes in the quality of your daily life.

Reading, Day 24

BECOME A YOGI

Who is a *yogi*? A *yogi* is one who understands the limitations of individuality, the falsehood of the personality. A *yogi* is one who understands the falseness of appearances and tries to penetrate reality. A *yogi* is one whose heart longs to be in union with the Cosmos. A *yogi's* heart melts at the suffering of others. A *yogi's* heart, the *yogi's* mind, is not clinging to selfish interests.

The *yogi* is one who is contemplative, who is meditative. The *yogi* is one who cultivates a positive, friendly mind; one who nourishes continual, living awareness of the full truth of his or her existence.

Through meditation, the *yogi* realizes what a great gift it is to be a human being. What an incredible gift it is to have a human mind! What a grace to have this wonderful, unique system of mind, heart, and soul, which can commune with Nature in totality, provided we keep the instrument properly tuned.

Regular practice is essential. Everyday practice. Practice. Practice. Practice. Practice being more awakened. Practice being more aware. Practice being more accepting. Practice becoming more conscious. Practice understanding the presentations of life that come to you. They come to you at every moment from the inherent, mysterious wisdom in the great flow of life, from an unknown, unseen Divine source.

Practicing consistently, we don't remember God only when we are in distress. We remember God, we remember grace, we remember the love which surrounds us, we remember and are grateful for all the gifts we have been given, at every moment.

We come to know what we have always known: the source is universal. The source is Divine. Our eyes can see only through the light of the Divine. Our ears can hear only through the light of the Divine. Our heart can beat only through the light of the Divine. Our being breathes, pulsates, and lives only through the Divine. God is the Doer.

The more you feel grace within every moment, the more you open yourself to it, acknowledging it in your prayers, in your words, in song, in chanting, in all of your practice and in your daily living, the more Divine energies and grace groom your mind.

Divine grace disciplines your mind, trains your mind, soaks your mind with pure love. One day, your mind melts. Your ego melts. Your ego becomes supple, humble, simple. Wisdom dawns in you.

It is the ego, our sense of separation from one another, from God, and all that is that is the obstacle to wisdom and to our essence. The more we surrender our ego, the more we allow Divine light to penetrate through us. We begin to recognize everything happening around us as the moving hand of grace.

What is needed is to practice making our mind our best friend. We need to befriend ourselves, to practice *yoga*, to practice union. To practice *yoga* is to be humble. It is to be simple. It is to be available to others, to be available to the highest energies of the Universe, to allow them to flow through us for the good of the world.

All the *yogis* of the world have said it time and again: Nothing can be achieved until and unless you open your heart and surrender yourself to the higher power of the Divine. Nothing can be healed until and unless you acknowledge the magnitude of your own limitations and seek that power, that love, that compassion which is infinite.

Nothing can change for us until and unless we reckon with the limitations of individuality by which each of us is separated from the Indivisible Cosmic Consciousness. Until and unless we recognize that it is this separation from the Cosmos, this separation from the living whole of Consciousness that is the root of all our miseries, there is no escape from suffering.

Ignorance creates all separation. Until and unless we pierce our ignorance of the nature of individuality, we remain shrouded, clouded, and imprisoned by a mind that identifies with this tiny body. That is the bottom line of all the agonies of our lives.

Until and unless we understand this deeply, true spiritual awakening cannot happen. As long as we are sensually bound, as long as we are emotionally bound, grace cannot flow through us.

We create the obstructions in our life. We create our own miseries. We can also create happiness for ourselves. We cannot make anyone or any situation responsible for our unhappiness. We need to bring all the focus to our individual self to find out what the larger, infinite Self is all about.

It is in the mind that we are bound. It is in the mind where we can be totally freed. It is in the mind where we feel bondage and pain. It is in the mind, also, where we can feel bliss, the joy of true freedom.

If we open ourselves, if we acknowledge that this human birth, this human body, this whole human existence has a deeper purpose to uncover, we find the path to freedom. The more we remind ourselves of that deeper purpose, the more we move toward Unity.

Every time you do good, all goodness dawns in you, all goodness comes into you. That is the message of the mind that is your best friend. It is the message of the *Gita*. It is the message of *yoga*. It is a simple message of awakening. It is the message of your own spirit, your true Self.

We all are born to awaken. We are born to awaken from the slumber of our unconsciousness, to awaken from our ignorance which is the root cause of all unhappiness. We are all born to fulfill our own nature and our nature is Divine. Grace is eternally available to all of us. No small effort toward awakening goes in vain. Brick after brick, each step takes us toward the mansion of our true, Divine home.

Practice

1. Spend some time in silence each day. Find a quiet, peaceful place. Sit comfortably erect. Relax your body from head to foot, focusing on relaxing each body part. Then take a few deep breaths. Inhale deeply and exhale deeply. Breathe consciously, withdrawing from external perceptions. Watch the flow of universal energy, *prana*, moving in and out

through your nostrils. You are consciously connected with the *vishwa-prana*, the universal life force that sustains all life. Feel the beautiful rhythm of your life flowing through the breath.

2. Thoughts will come and go to take you away from your concentration. Don't condemn your thoughts. Don't condemn yourself. Just relax. Bring your focus back to your breath and keep breathing. Let your thoughts go into the rising and falling of the breath. Experience lightness in your body, calmness of mind, and peace in your heart. Pray for Divine love alone.

3. Come out of meditation gradually, bringing your mind to the body. Thank God for the gift of your wonderful body and mind. Relax, bring your consciousness to the external world and feel all is well in your life. Bless everything around you when you open your eyes. Celebrate and be joyful for this gift of meditation and your union with all that is.

Reading, Day 25

THE WAY TO GOD IS THROUGH YOUR OWN NATURE

It is necessary that the seeker of truth contemplate the Self. You must discover your own nature. The way to God, the way to happiness, is through your own nature. Accepting your nature, respecting it, flowing with it, your life is in balance. Working with your nature, you avoid creating unnecessary resistance. Your life moves forward naturally and harmoniously.

Human beings travel through different *gunas*, prime qualities of the mind. We move from the lower *tamasic,* to the higher *rajasic*, to the highest illumination of the *sattwic.* Everything depends on the vibrational frequency, the level of awareness of the individual seeker.

There is nothing to judge. It is simply a matter of who is in what part of the process in the various arenas of life. According to the individual's nature, one treads the path toward final Unity.

What is the pull of your own nature? To study one's own nature at close proximity makes the path easier. If you are a person who is *rajasic*, you have a very active mind. You have lots of ambitions, lots of things to achieve, lots to do, many unfulfilled desires cramming your mind. You feel they are your first priority. You have to do, do, do. A lot of force, a lot of energy and activity are involved.

For such an active, dynamic mind, the path of *karma yoga* is best. A *sattwic* path of pure meditation, of sitting in contemplation for long periods of time, would be extremely difficult. It would be forced. *Karma yoga* is more natural, doing everything with dynamism, with enthusiasm, while searching for the true Doer of all actions.

One who is *rajasic* in nature only has to become more alert; more conscious in performing the actions of the day-to-day; more and more conscious of the Doer within, the God within as well as the God without. The seeker closely observes and asks: Are these actions driven by the desires of my ego? Are they sincere offerings of my heart to please and serve the Divine? Are they motivated by selfish concerns or by selfless dedication? What is the force behind my motivation?

God looks to the motivation of what we do and what we think. It is our attitude, our motivation, the energy of our being that becomes important rather than what we do.

Even mundane activities of a *rajasic* person gradually become focused on the Divine Doer in the course of becoming more focused, conscious, and aware of the Divine potential within. The Divine is ultimately the source of all thoughts, the source of all actions, the source of all energies, the source of consciousness. The more we become aware of this, the more we grow on the path of spirituality.

A person who has grown beyond this active, hectic, dynamic life has seen enough of it and doesn't find any charm in it anymore.

For that *sattwic* seeker, the pull is toward a more contemplative, simple, humble life of surrender. Push that person into a lot of activity and he or she will not show much interest. It is not his or her nature.

There is a very subtle difference between a *sattwic* person and a *tamasic* person, though they may look alike. A *tamasic* person will try to avoid work. He or she will try to avoid activity and escape responsibilities. More influenced by lower forces, a *tamasic* person is unstable, docile, and passive.

A person who is *sattwic* might appear to be a person who is not interested in an active, ambitious life, but that person has a stable and harmonious mind. He or she understands reality more deeply than a *rajasic* or *tamasic* person.

A *sattwic* person chooses food, literature, company, endeavors and surroundings that promote consciousness and unity with the Divine. The *sattwic* person gravitates toward what helps the Divine to unfold rather than the ego. The *sattwic* devotee tries to move ahead, to free himself or herself from the ego's domination. The *sattwic* person is more surrendered to the Divine will and Divine love. He or she accepts life in its totality, without resistance, without judgment, without reaction.

Yes, you can generalize. There appear to be two doors through which to enter the Kingdom of God. One is through the head, through reason. The other is through the heart, through emotion. Though you may initially choose one due to your own nature, you inevitably must walk through the other. If you move through the heart, you come to realize the essence of wisdom. If you move through the head, the time comes when your wisdom is soaked in Divine love and ecstasy.

The head and heart are intermingled. They cannot be isolated one from the other. The path of discrimination, an analytical inner search for the Self, is always good. It is founded upon sound inner research.

Devotion gradually refines emotions. As long as your emotions cling to human beings or material objects, their focus is external. Contaminated with material identification, they easily become unbridled. They drain you. They cannot give you pure bliss, pure happiness. Though you may love, it is love for something in the world, something by its nature impermanent and imperfect. You can never attain peace through it. That is the nature of emotion given to anything impermanent. The same emotion, the same love, the same heart opened to the Divine in all beings, will gradually be refined and lead to Divine love.

With Divine love, you do everything for your Beloved. It is as if you are breathing for your Beloved, seeing for your Beloved, singing and listening, doing everything for the sake of your Beloved.

Your love permeates everything that is external to you. Those you touch feel touched by Divine love, without selfish motivation, without any sense of expectation or judgment. Love flows through you and comes back to you manifold, because the more you love, the more you are filled with love. The more you love the Divine, the more the Divine responds to your love.

Constant self-analysis — a very keen and neutral self-analysis about where your ego is dominating, where you are drawn to impermanence, where you seek happiness outside of your own being, where you are drawn unconsciously — is invaluable. If you are alert to discriminate and understand the play of your mind, then you are awakened in the path of *jnana*.

If, simultaneously, your emotions and your love are open to the Divine, to Divine will and grace, if you are seeking and searching and touching everything with that Divine, your emotions brighten. You become a beautiful blend of the head and the heart. They work in harmony with each other, supporting and strengthening each other. Your spirit lives in joy.

Gradually, the spirit is freed from the cage of the conditioned mind and distorted emotion, from intellectual fantasies. Given unconditionally to the Divine, you come closer and closer to yourself. Your being blooms in its fully realized nature as you move toward Self-Realization. You realize that you are not separate from your Beloved. You are not separate from your true Self. You and your Beloved are one. That is the purpose of human birth.

For all human beings, the path is through the head, through the heart, to the Divine.

Practice

1. A great Himalayan Yogi who lived for a hundred and sixty years gave a wonderful practice in order to know what kind of nature you truly have:

At night when you retire to bed, when everything is calm and you have done your day's work, instead of just falling into bed and going to sleep, sit down on the bed. In a deep mode of contemplation and surrender to the Divine, let your mind go. There are no external disturbances. You can focus on your mind and see where it goes of its own accord. What thoughts and images arise? Try not to judge. Let go. Let the mind go. Let it fly. Let it move where it will.

You will experience the mind coming to certain points again and again and again. You will see that there are certain dominant processes in the mind.

2. Repeat this exercise the next day also. Repeat it often when you are going to bed. Practice this. Let go of the mind. Allow it to float in a way that you observe it, without

judgment, to see where it is ultimately going. You can discover what types of thoughts, what kinds of preoccupations, your mind is gravitating toward. That is the pull of your nature.

Reading, Day 26

OBSERVING YOUR MIND WITHOUT JUDGMENT

To monitor your mind and thoughts, it is important to be neutral, to observe your thoughts without categorizing them. When you put things into categories of good or bad, you are being judgmental. Anything you identify as bad only becomes more powerful. We see that clearly in children. When you ask a child not to do something, it becomes almost irresistible to the child.

Your mind is nothing more than a child's mind. It resists any restrictions, any imposition from outside, because it loves freedom. It has been given freedom. A sudden withdrawal of freedom is never accepted or appreciated. The less judgmental you are toward your mind, the less condemning you are, the less resistance you have, the better your mind will perform, the more cooperative and harmonious it will be.

Most people battle with the mind in meditation and in their daily work. They find what is wrong with themselves, how many mistakes they have made. They keep a running list. Then the pattern extends to others.

Anything that brings about self-condemnation is not a spiritual path. While it is good and helpful to recognize mistakes, repeating that you have made this or that mistake doesn't send your mistakes away. Those who repeat a mantra of "sin, sin, and more sin" get caught in the morass of sin.

Anything you observe keenly calms down. If you give your full attention to your hand or leg, or to a pain, after you observe it for some time, it becomes quiet. This is the nature of consciousness and of unconsciousness. Anything you do unconsciously persists as long as you are unconscious. The moment you observe it and become conscious about it, it stops. Try it. Try it in your life for some time, without categorizing, without judging.

Thoughts are thoughts. Good and bad are definitions of your conditioned mind. You are already suffering from this condition of the mind. All of your suffering is from the conditions of the mind.

Becoming more watchful, more vigilant of your mind at play, you watch what kinds of thoughts are coming and going. Be compassionate. Be understanding toward yourself. If you don't love yourself, you can't love God. You certainly can't love others.

The love of God happens only through love of the true Self. Any extreme self-criticism leads to suffering, to depression. Then you don't achieve much. Years roll by. You have been on the path of spirituality. You have been practicing this. You have been practicing that. You have been doing this *yoga*, that *yoga*, this meditation, that technique, but substantially, not much happens.

A *yogi* is in an unconditioned state. All others are in a conditioned state. A *yogi* is one who is no longer under the compulsion of any conditions. A *yogi* is one who never discriminates. His or her mind is free of conditions. The common person would discriminate between the water of the drain and the water of the Ganges, because his or her mind has been preconditioned that this is drain water, nasty. That is Ganges water, holy. These distinctions, these judgments, are conditions of mind. In a pure state of mind, these conditions no longer linger. To the saint, it is all God; it is all holy.

For an ordinary, conditioned soul, we have our definitions. We have our categories. We have our priorities. We have preferences. We have our own concepts, our thoughts. As we move higher and higher, these conditions gradually dissolve. As these conditions dissolve and as you become more and more unconditioned, you find that your devotion, your love, your surrender are becoming purer and purer.

Conditions are the impurities of the mind. In the Hindu tradition, the *satguru,* the true spiritual teacher and guide of the soul, gives a tremendous gift to the disciple. He deconditions the child, the disciple. He creates situations by which the disciple is gradually forced to surrender all conditions. The concepts and preferences that were so dear lose their grip. The disciple finds that they mean nothing. What comes to have true meaning is the will of God.

All prayers and spiritual practices are basically to purify the mind, to decondition the mind, to empty the mind, so that the mind can be filled up by Divine grace, Divine grace, Divine grace. As sincere seekers, we start surrendering the conditions, the preconceived notions, the programs of the mind, at the altar of the sacred. One after the other, like oblations into fire, we offer them. With regular practice of this inner fire ritual, the mind is freed and purged of its impurities. The mind becomes the Divine Mind, the Cosmic Mind, the Universal Mind.

In the Universal Mind, there is no pain, there is no pleasure. There is no insult and there is no praise. There is no play of opposites. In the Universal Mind, nothing of that can play any more. It is only in the individual mind that all these habits can play.

The unconditioned mind is universal. In the unconditioned mind, *samadhi*, the state of conscious, ecstatic union with the Divine, becomes possible. In *samadhi,* you merge with the Infinite Divine.

Practice

1. Practice being non-judgmental, non-reactive, non-resistant. First, see what is happening to your mind. What are the thoughts that are coming into your mind? Watch your thoughts in a very compassionate meditation. You are separate from the thoughts. If you watch the thoughts and keenly observe them, you find each and every thought rising up, appearing for some time, then dissolving in no time, because you are not participating.

2. Practice observing your thoughts without engaging with condemnation or appreciation. Condemnation or appreciation is nothing but your energy being given to that thought. The energy of response forms and reinforces a memory in your mind. The memories then block the mind. If you witness without judgment, the thought comes and it dissolves.

It cannot impress itself on you. It came, because it was a part of you. It stayed, because it had to stay for some time. Its impression was not strong because it could not find cooperation from you. It received no reinforcing energy, so it fell away.

3. After you gain some skill in this, gradually begin to follow your thoughts. From where is this thought arising and evolving? Where is it dissolving? From where does it come and where does it disappear? This second stage follows the thought trails.

Eventually, automatically, even the thoughts that were coming at random will be less and less in number. You become focused on the thoughts without any judgment.

4. As you find where each thought is coming from, as you find where it lingers and where it disappears, you discover you have begun to flow with the thoughts. Now it is as if you are a surfer. You are surfing the webs of the mind.

Previously, you fought with the water, with the waves of the mind. You could not surf. You were crashing into the water, falling and being shoved to shore. Now, you know how to surf the waves. You are no longer fighting, no longer resisting. You are moving with the waves. You have separated yourself a little.

5. Ultimately, you find that you can even catch the gaps between thoughts. Normally, we cannot catch them. We are not aware of our thoughts. The more conscious we become about our thoughts, the more conscious we become of our mind. This consciousness of our thoughts gradually brings to us a calmer mind, because our mind is not random anymore.

Reading, Day 27

A WORD OF REASSURANCE

If you are practicing, there are going to be moments, there are going to be times, when you are forgetful. That, too, is part of the process. The pain of forgetfulness is also a part of your experience. It impresses itself on your mind. Gradually, you come to realize that your Self-forgetfulness, the forgetfulness of your Divine connection, is the reason for all your unhappiness. Otherwise, you would never long deeply for a Divine connection.

The muddle of your mind has not come one fine morning. There is a cause to this effect. It is the accumulation of thoughts and practices for many, many years in the past. Accept that human reality. If you are determined today to change it, if you practice every day to change it, you are assured by all the sages, by all the enlightened ones, that yes, by practice, you can alter this. You can reverse the process. If your practice was emotionally negative then, yes, your determination to make your mind your best friend can take you back to the positive within you.

All experiences of our day-to-day life, bitter or sweet, help us to realize that the ultimate solution comes only through spiritual longing. Solutions materialize provided we practice every day and remind ourselves, time and again. It is only through practice that we can realize the goal of our life.

What I would share with you is this: Intensify your practice. Take refuge in the Divine Name. Chant that Holy Name which is sweetest to your heart. Chant it more and more within you, in spite of the fact that you are restless in your mind. Don't worry about that.

It is understandable that you worry about mundane matters, but do not start worrying about your worship, your prayers!

Be more loving of yourself rather than condemning and finding fault with yourself. Rejoice in the little that you can do in spirituality. Feel happy that, yes, God has come into your life. There are moments of forgetfulness. So what? God is with you. The more you appreciate yourself, the more you will feel the blessings of the Divine.

The positive is within you. The moment you begin to glimpse the positive within you, it grows. It grows with your nurturing attention. You will come to feel that you are flooded with grace. Before that, you feel deprived. Before that, you feel that nothing is happening.

Nonetheless, everything is contributing to your awakening to your oneness with God. All the failures, all the negativity, all the tears are contributing to that final state of awakening. So accept the positive aspect of the process. Always refocus on the positive aspect of it. Rephrase the wording of your thoughts to build your strength and confidence. I have found this practice to bring tremendous benefit to those I have taught. Develop the positive energy within you. Repeat positive words in your mind. Speak positive words to the world and to your surroundings.

Surround yourself with beauty. Take time to be grateful for everything good that comes to you. You will grow in spiritual consciousness. You will feel more and more Divine energy coming to greet you. You will grow in confidence in this spiritual world.

Practice

1. Practice brushing away the negative emotions, the negative patterns and ruts you find yourself in. They are like parasites trying to live on your own energy. Imagine them as trivial, small insects crawling on your shoulder that you can simply flick away. That is what they are, mere insects. They are nothing in comparison to who you are in God, to the power of your spirit, to the measure of the grace that God and the Holy Ones are extending to you. You are One with God. Remind yourself of that again and again.

2. No matter how often you find yourself in a muddle, simply begin again. Brush the insect of the negative away, time and again, as the nuisance it is. Then focus on what is real, on the positive vibrations of your mind. God is within you. You have infinite light and grace

available to you. Gradually you will grow out of all conflicts and confusion.

Reading, Day 28

ACTIVE COMPASSION AND GLOBAL TRANSFORMATION

Making our mind our best friend, we deepen in the life of our spirit. Our consciousness expands and our feeling connection to all of the life around us naturally intensifies. It becomes impossible to live only for ourselves and our own happiness. We know and feel the inner treasure, the immense dignity and beauty of the promise that aches to be realized in every human heart. Our concern for others, for the quality of life available in our world, takes on new dimensions.

One of India's recent great saints, from Agartala, one of the northeastern cities of India, left the body in early 2007. Maa was the simplest of saints, a humble servant of God whose utter surrender led to her being totally absorbed in the Divine Mother. She was virtually illiterate, but her visions and conversations with the Divine Mother were constant. Nonetheless, Maa reached the point where she could not go on in the world. "Human beings are no longer human," she said to me. "They have forgotten who they are in their spirit. I can't bear living in such a world, where the degradation and suffering is so deep, where there are such rampant violence and atrocities. What I see coming for the world is more of it, such upheaval and incredible suffering. I can't bear it."

If we are sincere as we progress in the life of our spirit, the magnitude of the pain and human suffering that goes on in our world exerts a pull on us. Our love and compassion for others are called to action. We realize that we must find some way to serve the life of the world, some way to contribute to the positive energy of the world.

The issues facing humanity stir our soul to ask ever deeper questions. What are the solutions to the maladies, the collective human afflictions, whereby human beings create such a self-destructive process? What are the obstacles to those solutions? How can we intervene in the collective pain and pathology of our human experience? How can we individually and collectively work to encourage spiritual friendship? How can we bring light and love, harmony and understanding, and rekindle healing consciousness wherever we can? And since we cannot be everywhere, doing everything, addressing every human need, where do we feel most called to serve and to support those who are addressing the deepest human suffering with integrity, heart, and intelligence? What sacrifices can we make to support the good and important work in our world?

These are personal questions each sincere seeker must ask and examine in his or her heart. Our compassion has to be active. We are part of the whole. What wealth, what light and joy and well-being that we garner in life, we are meant to share.

We naturally share from our being, one-to-one, every day as we move through our lives. But we also search for some way to give back to the larger whole that has been so gracious and generous to us. We need to share our outer as well as our inner treasure to alleviate some of the suffering in the world if we ourselves are to be truly whole.

That is not to say that we all need to become teachers or claim in any way to be a master or a guru. There are so many masters in the world. Everywhere you look, in every field you find a master of this, a master of that, a guru of this, a guru of that. There is such a rush for it, a stampede to put oneself forward as one with all the answers, as one who has made it.

Where are the disciples? Where are the disciplined human beings? It is so much harder to be a disciple, an authentically humble servant of God, than it is to claim to be a master or a guru. What the world needs today is not more teachers, not more masters, but more humble servants of the Divine and of humanity.

It is important to realize that not everyone is meant to travel into the very heart of human darkness. To directly witness and work among the most intense brutality and human suffering, you have to be truly ready.

You have to prepare your own mind. You have to train your own mind to withstand the magnitude of the darkness that you will encounter. If you are not adequately prepared, you will be overwhelmed in your own spirit when confronting the extreme cruelty in which human beings engage.

What is needed is a culture of compassion. Our selfless acts of love, however small and intimate, are manifestations of the Infinite Spirit and its love for humankind. They are the rekindling spirit in motion, flowing forward in the time stream with vast powers of proliferation, with ineffable powers to awaken and to heal. If everyone committed to one additional act of compassion a day, even if it were only bringing a smile to the heart of another who is unhappy or afflicted, our personal and collective human consciousness would begin to expand. The seeds of a new human culture of compassion could take root.

For true and lasting change, whether in our individual or collective lives, we need the intervention of spiritual powers. Spirit is foundational to life. It is foundational to health and happiness. It is beyond the mind, yet charged with perfect intelligence, unlimited in its creative and generative capacities. Nothing in human life changes without the movement and transformational influence of spirit.

What is needed is a soul-centered life, not a self-centered life. What is needed is a compassion-centered life, a prayer-centered life, a spirit-centered life that transcends dogma.

A true culture of the spirit will always be an interfaith spirit. Human survival demands that we understand the essence of our personal religion and transcend the externalities of form, dogma, and belief to open-heartedly embrace the light and value of all traditions. Humanity can no longer afford to confine and divide itself in the small-minded religious life that is based on fear and division. We must flow toward the ocean of the One, the unifying spirit where all religions mingle in love, harmony, peace, and spiritual co-existence.

The purpose of religion is basically one of transcendence. In the oneness of spirit, a true Hindu has to be, by spirit, a devout Christian, a devout Buddhist, a devout Muslim.

In the oneness of spirit, we all belong to all religions of the world. Any true religion will always take us toward oneness.

There are many people of good will who are relentlessly working to alleviate human suffering. One thing that has been missing, though, is a concerted, sustained, and collective interfaith endeavor of the spirit. We need a larger quantum of spiritual energy to counteract the tsunami of negative forces at work in the world. Only if we move beyond our own individual religious affiliation and join hands with all other faith traditions will humankind be able overcome the dark forces at work on the planet.

It is not by fighting terrorists that we stop terrorism. It is by creating deeper human regard, by creating more powerful healing energy in the atmosphere in which we all live and breathe. Then those who are rooted in dark forces naturally grow toward a gradual transformation from within.

Collective prayer and collective meditation offer immense potential for global transformation. They trigger and focus the higher powers and energies of collective consciousness to become a mighty force, one that is irresistible to God. Who knows what might happen if more of us joined hands and hearts and heads in group prayer more often, across the boundaries of our faith traditions, to ask for Divine intervention in transforming the human condition and moving our world toward peace and harmony.

Practice

1. Resolve to find an opportunity for at least one additional act of compassion a day.

2. When following through with this new practice, notice how the quality of your day is affected. Notice any impact on your consciousness that these compassionate exchanges have. What are you giving? What are you receiving? What more do you want to give?

3. If you are a member of a faith community, explore how you could encourage gatherings with other faith communities to pray for the world.

Reading, Day 29

SERVING THOSE WHO SUFFER IS SERVING GOD

Whatever our efforts to uplift others, we do only a little. What we receive is huge, incomprehensible. We do not do a lot. We receive a lot.

All of those who visit our street schools on the footpaths of Calcutta say the same thing. The children we serve are homeless. These children were born on the streets. They grew up on the streets. Their life is on the streets. When you meet them, when you talk to them, when you play with them, the language that they share with you through their hearts becomes your deepest memory of India. These children will be imprinted in your mind. You will have seen a new dimension. You will have seen God in a human face. You will have met God in another human heart.

There can be beauty and joy in the midst of poverty. There are many agonies in the midst of affluence. I have seen this time and again in my life, working with street children in India and during my travels around the world among rich and successful people.

We come to know life more closely if we visit and participate in works of deep compassion. Our heart expands and in that expansion our spirit blooms. The ego melts. We come to see the importance and the joy of being a direct instrument, of doing what little we can do for others.

Whatever helps us to expand moves us into a deeper experience of life. Contraction pushes us into misery. Contraction is the soil for all the agonies of our life. Direct works of loving compassion are a platform from which you work to free yourself from bondage, from all attachments, by growing in love. You expand in compassion. Smallness falls away.

What is compassion? Compassion is the melting heart of the Divine Mother in service to Her children. When you experience compassion in your heart or in the heart of another, know that it is God's heart melting in the human heart. You allow God to melt in your heart so that compassion can flow through you to touch every other soul.

There is never a question of personal credit or discredit in true service. You have become the vehicle through which God's compassion, God's love, God's life is expressing itself. You are a surrendered soul — a small, tiny child in the hands of the Divine. You have no worries. You cry when you are hungry. You desire, demand whatever you want. The Divine Mother is there always providing. Why worry? Once you learn the art of trusting and surrendering, your burdens become increasingly light. You discover that what was difficult to achieve through your own effort becomes easy whenever you do your best and entrust the rest to the Divine.

Ultimately, the role of all world religions, the role of all spiritual practice, is to support us in becoming good human beings. First and foremost, we need to become good human beings, people who uncover and express the goodness of our hearts. That is essential. It is what spiritual practice is about.

Practice

1. Find a new way to contribute to another human being each day, to practice generosity of mind and heart. Notice how that expands your experience of the goodness and beauty of life, how that carries the feeling and spirit of your day forward.

2. Extend the practice of compassion in your spiritual life beyond your immediate circle of self, friends, and family. Find new venues of compassion through which to express your love for God by serving the living God in those who suffer.

Reading, Day 30

BLESSING FOR YOUR JOURNEY FROM DEATH TO IMMORTALITY

There is a special manifestation when you have truly surrendered to God and made your mind your best friend. You are at ease. There is no dis-ease. You are at ease with yourself. Yes, disease will come to the body. Disease will go from the body. Yes, death will come to the body. But there is no disturbance, whatever comes. You remain untouched, unscathed, like the sky.

Such a life we can say is a Divine life. It has been moving with steady devotion from the lower to the higher, from ignorance to the ultimate wisdom of enlightenment. From fear of death, it has been moving with ever deepening trust in the Divine toward deathlessness and union.

May all the enlightened masters belonging to all faiths and traditions, whose Presence is eternal in the space in which we all live and breathe, bless us so that we can realize the unlimited expansion of the spirit. May their grace touch and open the lotus within our hearts.

When our heart is closed, we cannot help but become worldly. We are driven to substitute the unreal for the real. We acquire and acquire to escape our underlying distress and pain. We have the cataract of illusion obscuring our vision.

May infinite grace touch the lotus within our heart and all hearts.

May Divine light open the petals of the heart, one after the other. May we manifest our potential of Divine love for the whole universe through our human minds in harmony with the Infinite.

May our love expand to touch and envelop all hearts, all beings. May we realize that we are not this tiny little dot of an ego existence, this shadow. May we know that we are One. That is the reality that the sages of India announce so authoritatively, so boldly with the words: You are without birth and without death. You are THAT.

Practice

1. In prayer, invoke the power of infinite grace. Invoke all the powers of healing within you to express themselves, to flood the world with positive vibrations.

2. Feel and see, looking back over the time you have worked with these readings and practices, how you have been rediscovering yourself. How have you have come closer to who you truly are?

3. See and experience yourself as light in body and mind, with only befriending feelings for everyone. Appreciate and bless every aspect of your life, even the "negatives" of the past, as stepping stones toward befriending your own mind. Be grateful that life has been so infinitely kind to you by showing you the path to finding your one, true friend.

4. Beckon the friend of your own heart, the friend who will never leave you, the friend whom not even death can separate from you. This is your most intimate and loving friend, your positive mind that is in love with and at One with God.

5. Bless all beings on earth. Tell yourself again and again that all is well. Now you are set to experience the bliss of Divine Union, the perennial music of *yoga*, love Divine. Then close with the wonderful Vedic chant for the peace and happiness of all beings:

Sarve bhavantu sukhinah
(May all beings in this universe be happy)

Sarve santu niramayah
(May all beings enjoy sound physical
and mental health)

Sarve bhadrani pashyantu
(May we see good and auspiciousness in
each other and in everything)

Ma kaschit dukha bhag bhavet
(May no one be afflicted with misery
and unhappiness)

Om Shantihi, Om Shantihi, Om Shantihi.
(May peace prevail everywhere)

You may chant this regularly and after
each reading and practice.

ABOUT THE AUTHOR

Baba Shuddhaanandaa Brahmachari, more simply called "Baba," was born in Calcutta on May, 10 1949. At the age of twenty-six, he left an academic career in economics to become a monk. He has dedicated his life to serving the Divine and alleviating human suffering in all its forms. As the founder of Lokenath Divine Life Mission in India, Baba is held in the highest regard by the impoverished communities and populations which the Mission serves, by the Indian government and its agencies, and by the Indian press. He has been called "the pragmatic Swami" and the "No-Nonsense Swami" in the Indian press.

Baba is a practicing teacher of *Karma Yoga*. The essence of his teaching is based in the ancient Vedic principle of "Atma-Kripa," the grace of one's inner Self, which is achieved through love of the Self and expanding that to the unconditional love for all beings on Earth.

Wherever he goes, Baba translates ancient Vedic wisdom into simple, practical and effective tools for everyday living. He has a genius for getting at the root cause, the heart of any matter.

Through Lokenath Divine Life Mission, which Baba founded in 1985, Baba has worked relentlessly for the emancipation of impoverished women, children, and farmers in West Bengal, India. The Mission's development work is firmly grounded in principles of self-help. As a pioneer in the field of Micro Credit in the State of West Bengal, the Mission provides the ongoing training, education, and health services necessary for the poor to work with each other in improving their circumstances. That involves personal, heroic effort. Programs are designed so that those served will discover the magnitude of their own strength, character, and capacity to make a difference, not only in their own lives, but in the lives of others and that of their community.

Baba does not believe in traditional charity. He prefers to support people in liberating themselves rather than do anything to reinforce their sense of powerlessness.

Currently, more than 14,000 women participate in the Mission's 1300 self help groups. Annually, more than 270,000 people who would otherwise never see a doctor receive free medical care. More than 7,000 children receive free education. The Mission is also leading the State of West Bengal in forming Farmers Clubs to promote eco-friendly agricultural and village development.

Since 1990, Baba has been travelling and teaching regularly in the West. Among the occasions of his many lectures were the World Parliament of Religions (Chicago, 1993, and Barcelona, 2004), the Global Youth Conference (Washington, D C., 1993); World Hindu Conference (Frankfurt, 1992); the U.N. Millennium Peace Summit of World Religious and Spiritual Leaders (New York, 2000).

Baba's annual Global Tour regularly inspires thousands of spiritual seekers. He addresses the general public, corporations, and students at prominent colleges and universities across India, Germany, the U.K., and the

U.S.A., inspiring them with universal Vedantic teachings of Spiritual Oneness.

Other books in English authored by Baba are *The Incredible Life of a Himalayan Yogi*, a biography of his spiritual Master, Baba Lokenath; *Words of Pure Bliss*, a pocket companion/gift book on the spiritual journey; and *Creating Space for Celebration of Life: Clutter Free Home, Clutter Free Mind*. His talks on audio CDs are also a source of inspiration.

Recently, Baba has been addressing the increasing stress in our work and daily lives with his *Regeneration* seminars. Through his *Regeneration* seminars, corporate executives, police officers, government officials, students, health care providers, seniors, and prisoners are discovering the power within the body, mind and breath to restore their vitality, creativity, and peace of mind.

Baba lives in Kolkata (Calcutta) and Mumbai (Bombay) most of the year and tours the world to share the joy and bliss that is available to all human beings. He does not claim to be a guru. He has never formally initiated anyone into discipleship. Despite that, thousands love and respect him as their personal spiritual guide.

To learn more about Baba, his spiritual Master Baba Lokenath, and Lokenath Divine Life Mission, please visit:

www.feelinghearts.org

&

www.babalokenath.org

ALSO FROM BABA SHUDDHAANANDAA BRAHMACHARI

BOOKS

The Incredible Life of a Himalayan Yogi
Words of Pure Bliss
Creating Space for Celebration of Life: Clutter Free Home, Clutter Free Mind

MEDITATION MUSIC:

The Healing Meditation of "Om" – Chant by Baba

If you would like information on workshops, lectures, or other programs by Baba Shuddhaanandaa Brahmachari, or to order any of the books or audio CDs, please contact us at:

USA: www.feelinghearts.org
India: www.babalokenath.org

Baba invites you to write if you have anything to share about your journey to find your one true friend.

Stress Management Academy
24 Kali Temple Road,
Kolkata 700 026
Phone: 011+91+9831459958
email: shuvrom@hotmail.com
Or visit us at www.feelinghearts.org

2396042

Made in the USA